50 WALKS IN
Cornwall

50 Walks in Cornwall

Published by AA Publishing (a trading name of AA Media Limited, whose registered office is Fanum House, Basing View, Basingstoke, Hampshire RG21 4EA; registered number 06112600) Produced by AA Publishing

First published 2001
Second edition 2008
Third edition 2013
This edition 2019

Field checked and updated by Dixe Wills

Mapping in this book is derived from the following products:
OS Landranger 190 (walks 1–3)
OS Landranger 200 (walks 4–13, 42–43)
OS Landranger 201 (walks 44–50)
OS Landranger 203 (walks 15–31)
OS Landranger 204 (walks 14, 32–41)

ISBN: 978-0-7495-8116-9
ISBN (SS): 978-0-7495-7436-9

A CIP catalogue record for this book is available from the British Library.

Series management: Donna Wood
Editor: Liz Jones
Designer: Tom Whitlock
Digital imaging & repro: Ian Little
Cartography provided by the Mapping Services Department of AA Publishing

Printed and bound in Italy by Printer Trento SrL

A05661

We would like to thank the following photographers, companies and picture libraries for their assistance in the preparation of this book. Abbreviations for the picture credits are as follows:
Alamy = Alamy Stock Photo
12/13 travellinglight/Alamy; 39 Kevin Britland/Alamy; 55 Paul Martin/Alamy; 65 David Pick/Alamy; 79 steven gillis hd9 imaging/Alamy; 101 Kevin Britland/Alamy; 117 Seeables|Chris Rose/Alamy; 133 John Husband/Alamy; 155 Adrian Baker/Alamy; 169 Rob Cousins/Alamy

Visit AA Publishing at theAA.com

AA

50 WALKS IN
Cornwall

CONTENTS

The walks

HOW TO USE THIS BOOK

Each walk starts with an information panel giving all the information you will need about the walk at a glance, including its relative difficulty, distance and total amount of ascent. Difficulty levels and gradients are as follows:

Difficulty of walk

● Easy

● Intermediate

● Hard

Gradient

▲ Some slopes

▲▲ Some steep slopes

▲▲▲ Several very steep slopes

Maps

Every walk has its own route map. We also suggest a relevant AA or Ordnance Survey map to take with you, allowing you to view the area in more detail. The time suggested is the minimum for reasonably fit walkers and doesn't allow for stops.

Route map legend

_ _ _ ➔ _ _	Walk route	▢	Built-up area
❶	Route waypoint	▢	Woodland area
_ _ _ _	Adjoining path	🚻	Toilet
●	Place of interest	P	Car park
⌒	Steep section	▥	Picnic area
⚶	Viewpoint	) (	Bridge

Start points

The start of each walk is given as a six-figure grid reference prefixed by two letters referring to a 100km square of the National Grid. More information on grid references can be found on most OS and AA Walker's Maps.

Dogs

We have tried to give dog owners useful advice about how dog friendly each walk is. Please respect other countryside users. Keep your dog under control, especially around livestock, and obey local by-laws and other dog control notices.

Car parking

Many of the car parks suggested are public, but occasionally you may have to park on the roadside or in a lay-by. Please be considerate about where you leave your car, ensuring that you are not on private property or access roads, and that gates are not blocked and other vehicles can pass safely.

Walks locator map

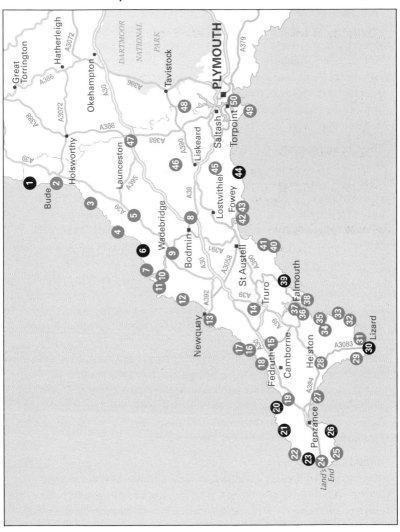

EXPLORING THE AREA

Cornwall's long, dwindling peninsula reaches out into the Atlantic like a ragged claw, and nowhere in that spit of land is more than 20 miles (30km) from the sea. The Cornish coast is traced by 268 miles (431km) of the South West Coast Path, which runs like a neat parting through maritime heathland and coastal fields, along the edges of dramatic cliff tops, and past magnificent beaches and picturesque fishing villages turned tourist resorts, such as Port Isaac, St Ives and Fowey. It is unsurprising, therefore, that Cornwall's extraordinary coastline is featured in a majority of the walking routes described in this book. In most cases, coastal walks in Cornwall can be linked with inland paths, tracks and lanes to provide satisfying circular walks, often with typically Cornish pubs, restaurants and cafés somewhere along the way.

The Cornish coast

There is hardly any part of the Cornish coast that is not exhilarating. On the north coast you are made dramatically aware of the vagaries of the sea and of its interaction with the land. This is a world of stupendous cliffs, of deep inlets and wave-lashed promontories, a world where Atlantic swells roll across acres of golden sand and where you can see the weather changing a mile offshore. Yet, on windless summer days, the cliff tops are gardens of wild flowers above a crystal clear sea.

On Cornwall's south coast, the cliffs can be just as compelling, though they are less barren and rugged and are spared the worst of Atlantic storms. Here, the quieter waters of the English Channel breed less tumultuous seas, the land is lush and green, and coves and beaches have a captivating serenity.

Many of the most picturesque stretches of the Cornish coast are in the care of the National Trust, whose commitment to sensibly managed access has furnished numerous linking footpaths that enhance the pleasure of coastal walking. This, together with the work of Cornwall's County, District and Parish councils, and with the co-operation of enlightened landowners and farmers, has seen a steady improvement in the upkeep of rights of way and in the development of permissive paths along the coast.

Inland Cornwall

The coastline is a hard act to follow, but inland Cornwall also has much to offer the walker. On Bodmin Moor, and on the Land's End Peninsula, paths lead through haunting landscapes, punctuated by the stone circles and burial chambers of prehistoric cultures. The woods of Cardinham and Calstock feel so landlocked that you would think the sea was a thousand miles away.

In Cornwall's towns and villages the distinctive character of this remarkable county is just as potent. Walk round Launceston, once the county town of an older Cornwall, and discover how much of its rich history is still reflected in the façades of old houses and in the medieval pattern of its streets. At Falmouth, enjoy the seagoing atmosphere of one of the world's biggest natural anchorages and one of Britain's most historic ports. At Polruan and Fowey, experience a palpable sense of how the sea, and a remote, secretive coastline, have shaped a colourful maritime past, when piracy and smuggling were part of the warp and weft of Cornish life.

Cornwall on foot

All of Cornwall's vivid contrasts are emphasised when you travel on foot, far from busy highways and the predictable round of tourist attractions. In the 'First and Last' county in England, there is a fresh perspective round every corner, a unique sense of place everywhere you walk. Exploring Cornwall on foot is to experience the best that walking can offer in a landscape that is like nowhere else in Britain.

PUBLIC TRANSPORT

Cornwall is well served by public transport, but you need to plan carefully if tackling the linear walks, for which it is helpful to combine a car with public transport. The main bus company in Cornwall is First Kernow. For timetable information for Walks 25, 40 and 49 telephone 0345 646 0707 or visit firstgroup.com. For rail enquiries (Walks 10 and 45) telephone 0345 700 0125 or visit gwr.com. For rail and bus information try traveline.info.

WALKING IN SAFETY

All these walks are suitable for any reasonably fit person, but less experienced walkers should try the easier walks first. Route-finding is usually straightforward, but you will find that an Ordnance Survey or AA walking map is a useful addition to the route maps and descriptions; recommendations can be found in the information panels.

Risks

Although each walk here has been researched with a view to minimising the risks to the walkers who follow its route, no walk in the countryside can be considered to be completely free from risk. Walking in the outdoors will always require a degree of common sense and judgement to ensure that it is as safe as possible.

- Be particularly careful on cliff paths and in upland terrain, where the consequences of a slip can be very serious.

- Remember to check tidal conditions before walking on the seashore.

- Some sections of route are by, or cross, busy roads. Take care, and remember that traffic is a danger even on minor country lanes.

- Be careful around farmyard machinery and livestock, especially if you have children with you.

- Be aware of the consequences of changes in the weather, and check the forecast before you set out. Carry spare clothing and a torch if you are walking in the winter months. Remember that the weather can change very quickly at any time of the year, and in moorland and heathland areas, mist and fog can make route-finding much harder. Don't set out in these conditions unless you are confident of your navigation skills in poor visibility.

- In summer remember to take account of the heat and sun; wear a hat and carry water.

- On walks away from centres of population you should carry a whistle and survival bag. If you do have an accident that means you require help from the emergency services, make a note of your position as accurately as possible and dial 999.

Countryside Code
Respect other people:

- Consider the local community and other people enjoying the outdoors.

- Co-operate with people at work in the countryside. For example, keep out of the way when farm animals are being gathered or moved, and follow directions from the farmer.

- Don't block gateways, driveways or other paths with your vehicle.
- Leave gates and property as you find them, and follow paths unless wider access is available, such as on open country or registered common land (known as 'open access land').
- Leave machinery and farm animals alone – don't interfere with animals, even if you think they're in distress. Try to alert the farmer instead.
- Use gates, stiles or gaps in field boundaries if you can – climbing over walls, hedges and fences can damage them and increase the risk of farm animals escaping.
- Our heritage matters to all of us – be careful not to disturb ruins and historic sites.

Protect the natural environment:
- Take your litter home. Litter and leftover food don't just spoil the beauty of the countryside; they can be dangerous to wildlife and farm animals. Dropping litter and dumping rubbish are criminal offences.
- Leave no trace of your visit, and take special care not to damage, destroy or remove features such as rocks, plants and trees.
- Keep dogs under effective control, making sure they are not a danger or nuisance to farm animals, horses, wildlife or other people.
- If cattle or horses chase you and your dog, it is safer to let your dog off the lead – don't risk getting hurt by trying to protect it. Your dog will be much safer if you let it run away from a farm animal in these circumstances, and so will you.
- Everyone knows how unpleasant dog mess is and it can cause infections, so always clean up after your dog and get rid of the mess responsibly – bag it and bin it.
- Fires can be as devastating to wildlife and habitats as they are to people and property – so be careful with naked flames and cigarettes at any time of the year.

Enjoy the outdoors:
- Plan ahead and be prepared for natural hazards, changes in weather and other events.
- Wild animals, farm animals and horses can behave unpredictably if you get too close, especially if they're with their young – so give them plenty of space.
- Follow advice and local signs.

For more information visit naturalengland.org.uk/ourwork/enjoying/countrysidecode

ALONG THE COAST FROM MORWENSTOW

DISTANCE/TIME	7.5 miles (12.1km) / 4hrs
ASCENT/GRADIENT	1,640ft (500m) / ▲ ▲
PATHS	Exposed cliff path with steep ascents/descents; inland paths and tracks can be very muddy during wet weather, many stiles
LANDSCAPE	High cliffs punctuated by deep grassy valleys and backed by quiet woods and farmland
SUGGESTED MAP	OS Explorer 126 Clovelly & Hartland
START/FINISH	Grid reference: SS205152
DOG FRIENDLINESS	Dogs on lead on cliffs and in fields
PARKING	Morwenstow. Follow signposted road from the A39 about 2.5 miles (4km) north of Kilkhampton to Morwenstow. Small free car park by Morwenstow Church and Rectory Farm Tea Rooms
PUBLIC TOILETS	Duckpool

The Gothic landscape of north Cornwall's Morwenstow parish, gaunt sea cliffs backed by remote farmland and wonderfully gloomy woods, was the ideal environment for the 19th-century parson-poet, the Reverend Robert Stephen Hawker, vicar of the parish from 1834 to 1874. He was devoted to his parishioners, most of whom were poor farmers and labourers, and also cared for the victims of shipwrecks on the savage Morwenstow coast. There were few survivors, and Hawker made it his duty to bury the dead. He would search the barely accessible foreshore beneath the cliffs, and salvage the often gruesome remains. Legend says that the vicar often dosed his reluctant helpers with gin to help them overcome their revulsion and superstition. The graveyard at Morwenstow pays homage to the drowned of numerous wrecks.

Hawker is said to have dosed himself with other substances too. He smoked opium, in keeping with the habits of fashionable Romantic poets such as Coleridge and de Quincy. At the tiny 'Hawker's Hut', a driftwood shack that nestles just below the cliff top near the beginning of this walk, he wrote and meditated, often under the influence. He is said to have dressed as a mermaid on occasions, took his pet pig, Gyp, for long walks, and once excommunicated a cat for catching a mouse on a Sunday. And why not?

Take the spirits of Parson Hawker and Gyp the pig with you through this dramatic landscape as you walk from the splendid Church of St Morwenna out to the edge of the great cliffs, to Hawker's Hut. From here the coast path dips into and out of dramatic valleys, often within sight of the slate-grey fins of smooth, slabby rock that protrude from the cliff edge. The route leads past the government's eerie radio tracking station at Cleve, where huge satellite receivers face the sky. At Duckpool, the cliffs relent and you turn inland and away from the often boisterous coast to find picturesque thatched cottages beside a placid river ford. Beyond lies the calm of deep woodland. The route winds through lonely fields and past handsome old manor houses at Eastaway, Stanbury and Tonacombe to reach Morwenstow's welcoming pub and then Parson Hawker's handsome church once more.

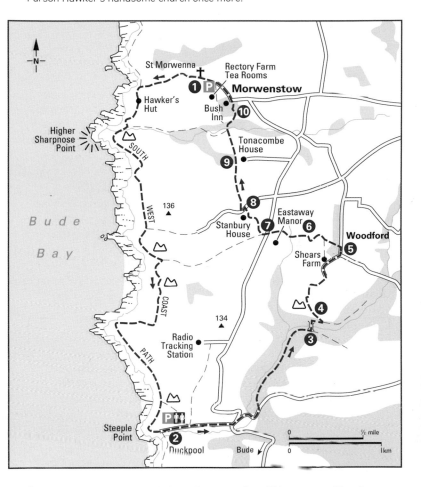

1. Follow the signposted track from the car park and Morwenstow Church to reach the coast path, then turn left. You'll reach Hawker's Hut in about 100yds (91m). Continue walking from here along the coast path to Duckpool.

2. When you reach the inlet of Duckpool, walk up the road along the bottom of the valley to reach a T-junction, and turn left. Bear right at the next junction to cross a bridge beside a ford. Follow the lane round to the left for about 150yds (137m), then bear off left along a broad track through some woodland.

3. After nearly 1 mile (1.6km), cross a stile on the left, go over a wooden footbridge, climb the slope, then turn right and up a track. Turn left at a T-junction, keep ahead at the next junction, then in 40yds (37m) carry straight on at a metal gate.

4. Follow a signed field track to a surfaced lane at Woodford. Turn left and go downhill past Shears Farm, then round right and uphill to a junction with a road. Turn left past a bus shelter.

5. After 100yds (91m), turn left along a path between cottages to reach a kissing gate. Turn right and then immediately left, and follow the edge of the field to a stile on the left. Cross the stile, then cross the next field to reach a hedge on the opposite side.

6. Go over two stiles and then straight up the next field, often muddy, to a hedge corner (left). Go alongside a wall and over a stile to a hedged track and on to a junction with a surfaced lane.

7. Go through a gate opposite, then turn right through a gap. Bear left across the field to a big Cornish stile. Keep straight across the next field to its top left-hand corner, then go through a gate up to Stanbury House. Turn right to reach a surfaced lane.

8. Go left along the lane for a few paces and then over a narrow stile on the right. Aim for a gap in the hedge opposite and go straight across the next two fields to reach a kissing gate into a farm lane behind Tonacombe House.

9. Keep ahead through a kissing gate, then along a track and through another. Cross two fields, then descend into a wooded valley via a kissing gate. Keep right, cross a stream, then go right (at a post signed 'Crosstown') and up steps to reach a kissing gate.

10. Ascend the field to reach the garden behind the Bush Inn. Go down the left-hand side of the buildings, then up to the road. Turn left for St Morwenna Church and the car park.

Where to eat and drink

The 13th-century Bush Inn is just along the road from Morwenstow Church. It does bar meals and you can enjoy a Cornish pasty with your Hick's Special Draught. The Rectory Farm Tea Rooms is at the start of the walk and from Easter to the end of October offers morning coffee, lunches, cream teas and evening meals by arrangement.

What to see

Revd Hawker's eccentricity extended to the vicarage he built next to Morwenstow church. The house's chimneys replicate the towers of other north Cornwall churches and the tower of an Oxford college. The kitchen chimney is a replica of the tombstone of Hawker's mother.

While you're there

Morwenstow's Church of St Morwenna is unavoidable and unmissable, from its atmospheric graveyard and splendid Norman doorways to its wonderfully gloomy interior. Even the approach to the lychgate has drama – note the visible depressions; these are the graves of unsanctified suicides or criminals. Just inside the gate, on the right, is a granite cross with the initials of Hawker's wife. The replica ship's figurehead on the left commemorates drowned sailors.

BUDE'S COASTAL GRASSLANDS

DISTANCE/TIME	5 miles (8km) / 2hrs 30min
ASCENT/GRADIENT	262ft (80m) / ▲
PATHS	Coast path excellent throughout, some inland paths overgrown in summer, several stiles
LANDSCAPE	Coastal cliffs, unstable in places; keep well back from cliff edges
SUGGESTED MAPS	OS Explorers 111 Bude, Boscastle & Tintagel and 126 Clovelly & Hartland
START/FINISH	Grid reference: SS204071
DOG FRIENDLINESS	Dogs on lead through grazed areas
PARKING	Crooklets Beach car park, follow signs for Crooklets. Large pay-and-display car park, can be very busy in summer. Sandymouth National Trust car park
PUBLIC TOILETS	Crooklets Beach, Sandymouth

The windswept coastal grasslands of north Cornwall seem unlikely havens for plant life but, around the seaside resort of Bude, the cliff edges especially provide a unique refuge for fascinating wild flowers. This walk follows the flat cliff land north of Bude, with an inland section on the return. Along the way you'll find numerous wild flowers that turn the cliff top into a riot of colour in spring and early summer.

The walk starts from the northern outskirts of Bude at Crooklets Beach, and within minutes takes you out onto the cropped grasslands of the National Trust's Maer Cliff and Maer Down. In spring the dominant flower here is the spring squill, whose distinctive powder-blue flowers are dotted across the grass. Other early plants which flourish here are the lilac-coloured early scurvy grass, the pink thrift and white sea campion.

At Northcott Mouth the cliffs give way to a wide, stony beach. Here the route of the walk turns inland and climbs steadily uphill to eventually follow the line of an old bridleway, often choked with a tangle of grass and brambles, but with typical hedgerow plants such as foxglove and red valerian poking through.

Soon you reach the road to Sandy Mouth Beach and the cliff path back to Crooklets. Once more there are many wild flowers here. The grass is laced with the yellow and orange flowers of kidney vetch and the yellow heads of hawkweed and, by July, is scattered with the pink and white florets of the aromatic wild carrot.

From Northcott the walk angles inland to a final stroll through an area of typically dense woodland, a dramatic contrast in habitat to the open cliff top. Here primroses and daffodils appear, brightening up the early spring. A mixture of trees such as sycamore, beech, alder, cypress, Scots pine and

Corsican pine create a sheltered and moist environment within which plants like the tall yellow flag iris and the lilac-coloured water mint thrive.

The last section of the walk leads you past the Maer Lake Nature Reserve, a large area of wetland that is flooded in winter and is in the care of the Cornwall Wildlife Trust and the Cornwall Birdwatching and Preservation Society. There is no public access to the area from the roadside, but you can get an excellent view of the many birds through binoculars.

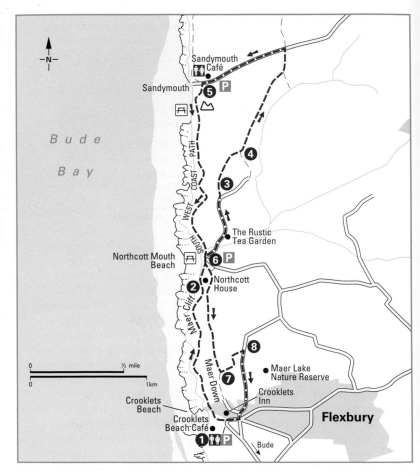

1. From the seaward end of Crooklets Beach car park (by the café), go towards the beach, turn right to cross a bridge and head for some steps. Pass behind some beach huts, then turn left along a stony track between walls. Go up some steps through a kissing gate and onto the coast path. Follow the coast path.

2. Go through a gate and then walk along a track behind a white building, called Northcott House. Bear off to the left, by a signpost, down a path to reach the sea at Northcott Mouth beach. From here, bear right along a track that will take you back inland, past a group of houses on the left, and continue uphill to pass The Rustic Tea Garden and scattered houses.

3. Where the track bends round to the right, leave it and keep straight ahead to an open gateway. Keep walking along a banked bridle path (skirt the field-edge to the left if the path is impassable).

4. Reach a field gate and follow a track through fields. Take the right fork at a junction with another track, then continue to a T-junction with a public road. Turn left and walk down the road, with care, to Sandymouth.

5. Pass the National Trust information kiosk and descend towards the beach, then go left and uphill and follow the coast path back to Northcott Mouth beach, and a lifeguard hut passed earlier on your route.

6. Follow the roadside path just past the lifeguard hut and then retrace your steps towards Northcott House, which you passed earlier. Go along the track behind the building and then keep ahead along a broad track with a field hedge on your left.

7. As buildings come into view ahead, turn left over a stile with a footpath sign in a wall corner. Follow the field-edge ahead into a hedged-in path. Continue walking between trees to a lane by a new house. Continue until you reach the road.

8. Turn right along the road, with Maer Lake Nature Reserve down to your left. Follow the road to a crossroads and turn right to return to the car park.

Where to eat and drink

There is a National Trust café (and toilets) in an attractive building at Sandymouth at the halfway point. Once seasonal, it is now open all year round. At Northcott Mouth, The Rustic Tea Garden (Easter to early October) has been offering light refreshments for 50 years. The Crooklets Beach Café and Rosie's Kitchen are passed at the start and end, as is Crooklets Inn.

What to see

Butterflies that are likely to be seen along the cliffs in summer include the meadow brown, probably Britain's most common butterfly, its name a perfect description of its dusky colour. Look also for the common blue, a small butterfly with an almost lilac tinge, and for the glamorous painted lady with its tawny orange wings and black and white markings. The painted lady's main habitat is Southern Spain and North Africa, from where large swarms often migrate north in April and May, finding no difficulty in crossing the English Channel.

GEOLOGY AT CRACKINGTON HAVEN

DISTANCE/TIME	4 miles (6.4km) / 2hrs
ASCENT/GRADIENT	270ft (82m) / ▲ ▲
PATHS	Good coastal footpath and woodland tracks; wet and muddy at times, several stiles
LANDSCAPE	Open coast and wooded valley
SUGGESTED MAP	OS Explorer 111 Bude, Boscastle & Tintagel
START/FINISH	Grid reference: SX143967
DOG FRIENDLINESS	Dogs on lead on cliffs and in fields; goats on cliffs south of Cambeak
PARKING	Crackington Haven car park from the A39 at Wainhouse Corner, or from Boscastle on the B3263; can be busy in summer. Burden Trust car park and picnic area
PUBLIC TOILETS	Crackington Haven

Crackington Haven has given its name to a geological phenomenon: the Crackington Formation, a fractured shale that has been shaped into incredibly twisted and contorted forms. On the sheared-off cliff faces of the area, you can see the great swirls and folds of this sedimentary rock that was metamorphosised by volcanic heat and contorted by the geological storms of millions of years ago. Even the name Crackington derives from the Cornish word for sandstone, *crak*. The very sound of the word, in English, hints at a dangerous friability and dramatic decay. Scripted across the face of the vast cliffs traversed by this walk are the anticlines (upward folds) and synclines (downward folds) that are so characteristic of these great earth movements.

During the 18th and 19th centuries Crackington Haven was a small port, landing coal and limestone and shipping out local agricultural produce and slate. Small coastal ships would anchor off the beach, or settle on the sands at low tide in order to exchange cargoes. Plans to expand Crackington into a major port were made in the early 19th century. The grandiose scheme aimed to build huge breakwaters to protect Crackington and the neighbouring Tremoutha Haven from the often huge Atlantic swells. Quays and docks were to be built inside the protected harbour. A rail link to Launceston was proposed and a small new town planned for the Haven, which was to be renamed Port Victoria. As with many development plans of the time, the scheme did not materialise, otherwise the Crackington Haven of today would be a dramatically different place.

As you set out along the open cliff south from Crackington, the remarkable nature of the geology unfolds before you. Looking back from Bray's Point, you can see clearly the massive contortions in the high cliff face of Pencannow Point on the north side of Crackington. Soon the path leads above Tremoutha Haven and up to the cliff edge beyond the domed headland of Cambeak. From here there is a breathtaking view of the folded strata and quartzite bands of Cambeak's cliffs.

The coast path leads to the tip of the headland, which is very exposed and not recommended in times of high wind and driving rain. The geology of the cliffs is still active, and one day erosion will destroy the neck of the headland, transforming Cambeak into an island, but preferably without you on it.

A short distance further on you arrive above the Strangles beach, where again you can look back towards such fantastic features as Northern Door, a promontory of harder rock pierced by a natural arch where softer shales have been eroded by the sea. Where the route of the walk turns inland there is a line of low cliffs set back from the main cliff edge. These represent the old wounds of a land slip where the cliff has slumped towards the sea. From here the second part of the walk turns inland and descends into East Wood and the peaceful Trevigue Valley, itself part of a great geological extravaganza, having once been a 'fjord' filled by the sea. Today much of the valley is a nature reserve, and wandering down its leafy length is a wonderful antidote to the high coastal drama of the Crackington cliffs.

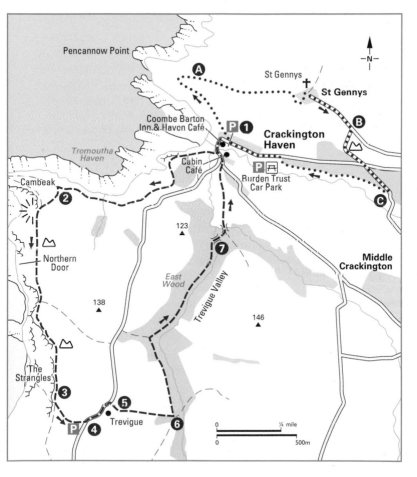

1. From the Crackington Haven car park entrance go left across a bridge, then turn right opposite the Cabin Café. Follow the coast path signs along a broad track to the left, past tennis courts and through a kissing gate. Fork right a few paces later.

2. Eventually a stile leads to a steep stepped descent to footbridges below Cambeak and a path junction. Keep left, signed High Cliff, and follow a path up a sheltered valley on the inland side of the steep hill, then continue on the cliff path.

3. At the start of a stretch of low inland cliff, turn left at a coast path post marked 'Trevigue' to reach a road.

4. Go left up the lane to reach buildings at Trevigue. Follow the lane left, then bear right down a drive alongside the house. Bear off to the left across the grass to go through a gate with a yellow arrow.

5. Go directly down the field, keeping left of a telegraph pole, to reach a stile. Continue downhill over a field to a stile on the edge of a wood. Continue down a tree-shaded path to a junction of paths in a shady dell by the stream.

6. Turn sharp left here, following the signpost towards Haven, and continue on the obvious path down the wooded river valley, ignoring a left turn to the coast road.

7. Cross a footbridge, then turn left at a junction with a track. Cross another footbridge and continue to a gate by some houses. Follow a track and then a surfaced lane to the main road, then turn left to the car park.

Extending the walk On returning to Crackington and waypoint 1, follow the road behind the Coombe Barton Inn for about 150yds (137m). Look out on the left for a coast path signpost beside a thatched cottage. From here the path rises unrelentingly to the top of the towering Pencannow Point. Take your time; the climb is surprisingly easy.

You are now perched above the awe-inspiring cliff seen from the main walk at waypoint 2. Pencannow is merely the root of a much higher land mass, worn down by millions of years of erosion. For the airiest of views you can follow a precarious path out along the narrow headland itself, but take care, especially when it is wet underfoot or there are strong winds blowing.

On the main route, follow the coast path, which leads sharply round to the right and then along the cliff edge to reach a kissing gate, Point A, into a cliff-top field. Just before the gate follow a sign inland to St Gennys to reach a kissing gate into another field. Follow the left-hand field-edge; eventually go through a kissing gate to reach St Gennys Church. The tiny settlement of St Gennys is crouched in a protective fold of the coastal hills. The church itself is a sturdy little building with traceable Norman origins.

Coming back up from the church, turn left and follow the lane, then go right at the second junction, Point B. Descend steeply to reach the main road. Cross the road with care and continue downhill. Go over a stone stile on the right, Point C, signposted to Crackington Haven, and onto a woodland path. This is the beginning of 'Lovers' Lane', a path that wends its romantic way along leafy tracks and above river meadows to reach the main road into Crackington Haven and the main walk's start point.

Where to eat and drink

The Coombe Barton Inn at Crackington Haven has spacious bars and a children's room, and serves a good selection of food and drink. There are also two cafés, one to either side of the car park entrance in Crackington Haven.

What to see

The field and woodland section of this walk supports a very different flora to that found on the heathery, windswept cliff land. Some of the most profuse field-edge and woodland plants belong to the carrot family, the *Umbelliferae*. They may seem hard to distinguish, but the commonest is cow parsley, identifiable by its reddish stalk, feathery leaves and clustered white flower heads. Hogweed is a much larger umbellifer, often standing head and shoulders above surrounding plants; it has hairy stalks and broad-toothed leaves and can cause an unpleasant rash if it comes in contact with your skin. A third common umbellifer is the Alexander, prolific in spring and early summer. It has broad, lime green leaves and clustered yellow florets.

While you're there

At waypoint 3, where the route turns inland, you can continue along the coast path for a few paces to where a path leads down right to the Strangles beach. Until well into the 20th century such beaches were a source of seaweed and sand for use as fertiliser on local fields. The track down to the beach gave access for donkeys. A visit to the beach is worthwhile, in spite of the steep return. You can view the remarkable coastal features from sea level.

TINTAGEL AND
TINTAGEL CASTLE

DISTANCE/TIME	3 miles (4.8km) / 2hrs
ASCENT/GRADIENT	197ft (60m) / ▲
PATHS	Good coastal paths and field paths, many stiles
LANDSCAPE	Spectacular sea cliff quarries
SUGGESTED MAP	OS Explorer 111 Bude, Boscastle & Tintagel
START/FINISH	Grid reference: SX056885
DOG FRIENDLINESS	Dogs on lead through grazed areas
PARKING	Several car parks in Tintagel
PUBLIC TOILETS	Tintagel; Trebarwith Strand

Tintagel, and its ruined castle on the spectacular headland known as the Island, is the centre of a resilient King Arthur industry based on Victorian romanticism and a few scraps of historical wishful thinking. It is thronged with visitors for much of the year, but this walk quickly leaves the crowds behind and crosses quiet fields to reach the magnificent coastline where there is plentiful evidence of, some may say, the real 'kings' of the Tintagel area: the coastal quarry workers who extracted slate from the great cliffs. Their reign lasted from medieval times until the early 20th century. There is evidence of quarrying from the Lanterdan Pinnacle to Penhallic Point, where a secure timber platform once projected from the cliff edge. Trimmed slates were lowered from the platform to cargo ships at the base of the cliffs. From Penhallic Point the coast path leads past a series of cliff-side workings at Gull Point Quarry and Lambshouse Quarry. At these quarries men were lowered down the cliff face on ropes to work out good slate from just above the tideline.

A visit to Tintagel Castle is hard to resist, not least for its spectacular position perched on 300ft (90m) cliffs. The ubiquitous King Arthur apart, the site was the stronghold of the medieval Earls of Cornwall, and probably of Bronze Age and Iron Age peoples too. Archaeological evidence suggests that it was occupied by a figure of great importance until the 8th century, when it was abandoned. Reginald, Earl of Cornwall, carried out construction work in the 9th century, but most of what remains today dates from the 13th century, when the site was massively refortified under Richard, Earl of Cornwall. Tintagel Castle is under the care of English Heritage and is open all year; it can be accessed from the upper entrance, passed on waypoint 7, or from the lower entrance on Tintagel Haven.

Although some believe that King Arthur was born here – Cornwall is peppered with sites claiming a link to him – there is no evidence. Arthur is likely to have been a powerful warrior, famed for his opposition to Saxon invaders, rather than a 'magical' king supported by the wizard Merlin. Barras Nose, the headland lying immediately to the northeast of the Haven, is renowned as the National Trust's first English coastal acquisition, in 1896.

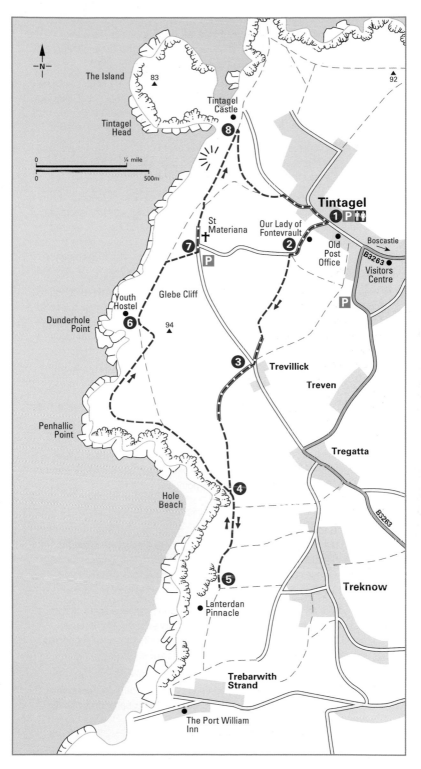

The Island

▲ 83

Tintagel Head

Tintagel Castle

❽

0 ¼ mile
0 500m

St Materiana

❼

P

Our Lady of Fontevrault

❷

Old Post Office

Tintagel

❶ P 🚻

Boscastle

B3263

Visitors Centre

P

Glebe Cliff

Youth Hostel

Dunderhole Point

❻

▲ 94

❸ Trevillick

Treven

Penhallic Point

Tregatta

B3263

Hole Beach

❹

Treknow

❺

Lanterdan Pinnacle

Trebarwith Strand

The Port William Inn

—N—

▲ 92

1. Leave the bustle of Tintagel by turning left down Vicarage Hill alongside the Cornishman Inn, signposted 'Parish Church – Glebe Cliff'. Descend steeply, passing the 14th-century Chapel of Our Lady of Fontevrault (left).

2. Where the rising lane turns sharply right, leave the lane and go over a stile. Bear slightly right to a gate and stile, then go through the next field, bearing right to a stile. Continue on a fenced path along the right-hand edges of small fields to reach a track. Follow the track to a junction of tracks at Trevillick.

3. Keep straight across, signposted 'To the Coast Path'. Pass two houses and keep ahead to where the track ends at a field gate and stile by final houses. Cross fields ahead to reach a junction with the coastal footpath.

4. Go left along the coast path for a short distance to reach a junction with a track. From behind a wall you can look down at the Lanterdan Pinnacle, a tower of uncut rock rising to 80ft (24m) left in place because of its inferior slate. (The route returns north from here, but you can continue along the coast path from Lanterdan Quarry for 0.5 miles (800m) to descend to Trebarwith Strand; it's a steep climb back up to rejoin the main walk.)

5. Retrace your steps from above Lanterdan Quarry to where the path followed from Trevillick joins the coast path. Follow the coast path to eventually cross a stile and reach a gap in a wall on Bagalow Cliff. Turn left here, go over a stile then follow the path round Penhallic Point to join a broad track that leads down to Tintagel Youth Hostel, once the offices of the nearby cliff quarries.

6. Go past the hostel, then follow the coast path with the Church of St Materiana in sight (see While you're there). Bear right towards the church.

7. Turn left and follow a track along the seaward wall of the churchyard. Keep on this path towards the headland of the Island to cross a stile on the coast path; descend past fortifications to reach the upper approach to the castle.

8. Keep ahead here if you want to visit the castle, or turn right and follow a valley-side path to reach the road (and later path) that leads steeply uphill to Tintagel. Turn right to return to the start point.

Where to eat and drink
Along the coast path from Lanterdan Quarry to Trebarwith Strand you will find the Strand Café and The Port William Inn. Tintagel Castle Beach Café is at the lower entrance to the castle.

What to see
The whole area above the quarries and inland has stone walls of slate laid in herringbone pattern and known locally as curzyway. Keep an eye out for the old platforms at the top of the cliffs that once supported wooden gantries used for lowering slates to ships below.

While you're there
The Church of St Materiana is just inland from the cliffs, but deserves a visit. It dates chiefly from the 12th century but probably occupies the site of a much earlier Christian oratory.

EXPLORING CAMELFORD
AND BEYOND

DISTANCE/TIME	5.5 miles (8.8km) / 3hrs
ASCENT/GRADIENT	164ft (50m) / ▲
PATHS	Obvious, well-marked paths, some field sections poorly defined; many stiles, some in triplicate and very high
LANDSCAPE	Wooded riverside, fields and quiet lanes
SUGGESTED MAP	OS Explorer 109 Bodmin Moor
START/FINISH	Grid reference: SX106836
DOG FRIENDLINESS	Dogs on lead through fields; may find high, multiple stiles difficult
PARKING	Church car park (free) at north entrance to Camelford, or small car park opposite the defunct North Cornwall Museum & Gallery
PUBLIC TOILETS	Entrance to Enfield Park, Camelford, near church car park. Car park opposite the defunct North Cornwall Museum & Gallery

Camelford nestles in a river valley on the western side of Bodmin Moor. It has a long and distinguished history, having originated as a strategic river crossing that was granted a Royal Charter as early as the 13th century, giving it the right to hold markets and fairs. The old coaching road to the west skirted the raw uplands of Bodmin Moor and passed through Camelford. Today the town retains its strong historical character, despite incessant through-traffic.

The start of this walk delivers you instantly into leafy riverside shade and peace and quiet. From Camelford's town hall you cross the narrow Fore Street and pass through an arched passageway called 'The Moors', another indication of an older Camelford that had immediate references to the great sweep of Bodmin Moor to the east. Here it is all wooded riverside paths that take you downstream alongside the River Camel. After 0.5 miles (800m) or so the route climbs away from the river through quiet meadows, and a wonderful trout pond garden at Trethin, to reach the handsome Advent Church of St Athwenna. The church has a flourishing breeding colony of rare brown long-eared bats.

From the church the route leads through fields and along quiet lanes with unexpected views of the dragon-backed rocky ridge of Roughtor (pronounced Rowtor) and its higher neighbouring hill, the more rounded Brown Willy, the highest point in Cornwall at 1,378ft (420m). At Watergate, you pass through an intriguing area of old walls and terraces that may have been part of a mill complex; today the walls are muffled with velvety moss, and the ground is thick with lush grass. Soon higher ground is reached at Moorgate, another name echoing the area's domination by Bodmin Moor. From here you then head back towards Camelford, passing along some engagingly muddy lanes on the way.

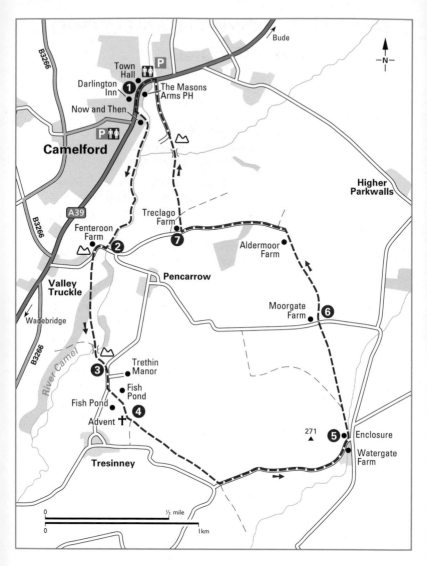

1. From the pavement opposite the town hall, walk up Fore Street past the Darlington Inn for 50yds (46m). Go left through an archway signed 'Riverside Walk'. Follow the riverside path across a footbridge and downstream.

2. At a surfaced lane and beside a bridge, turn right and uphill. At the top of a steep incline, just past Fenteroon Farm, go left and through a gate, signposted 'Public Footpath'. Follow the fenced path along the field-edge and across the next field. Go over a very high stile and descend through woods towards the river. Ignore the stile on the right and keep down left to a signpost in the valley bottom. Cross the meadow ahead, then go left over a bridge and bear right through a tangle of trees. Bear steeply up left to pass a footpath post and gate. Keep uphill to reach a stile into a lane.

3. Turn right, then, just past the entrance to Trethin Manor, bear off left over a stile, and go through a pleasant garden and orchard and past a fish pond. Cross a granite clapper bridge and a stile, then go up the field to Advent churchyard, entering via a stile and gate. Tea, coffee and squash are available in the church.

4. From the east end of the churchyard (on the opposite corner) go through a metal gate and over a wooden stile and bear half right across a field to three stiles in quick succession. Cross two fields then follow the right-hand field-edge to three stiles in the hedge. Bear left across the middle of the next field to its far corner and over two stiles on to a surfaced lane. Turn left.

5. Turn left just before the stream and T-junction by Watergate Farm. Go over two stiles and alongside the stream on stone flags. Pass a little enclosure, follow the stream for a short distance, then bear left to skirt high gorse; then bear right downhill to pick up the path over stiles into a field. Keep in the same direction, climbing gently, to find a stile into the next field. Bear half-left, having swerved around the morass of impenetrable grasses, to reach the lane at Moorgate Farm, aiming for a kissing gate between buildings.

6. Cross the lane. If the right of way across a high bank is impassable, go through the farm entrance and cross a stile to the left of a barn. Keep ahead across two fields and along the left edge of a third, then continue along a stony track through fields to reach another lane at Aldermoor Farm. Turn left along the lane, eventually reaching Treclago Farm.

7. Just before the farmhouses, on the right, turn right up a track, as signed by a faded guidepost propped against a stone barn. Soon, at a junction of tracks, head straight on. This section can be very muddy. Descend to a gate and head down a meadow to a gate and stile. Cross a wooden footbridge over a stream, then climb steeply uphill to reach a surfaced lane. Follow the lane, College Road, to reach Camelford.

Where to eat and drink
Camelford has many food outlets. The Masons Arms and the Darlington Inn both do bar meals.

What to see
Look out for the dipper, a small dark brown bird with a white patch on its breast. It can stay under water for a time, braced against the stream's flow while seeking out aquatic insects, water snails, larvae and even tiny fish. It can also 'swim' under water, using its wings.

While you're there
Visit the Now and Then Museum on Fore Street for an insight into Camelford life in the past and present. Walk down Chapel Street with its cobbled rainwater gullies, and look at the town's historic buildings such as the town hall with its golden camel weather vane. Nearby Darlington Inn has 16th-century features, and although the interior was destroyed by fire in 1995, much has been restored. At the north end of Market Place is the attractive Enfield Park.

PORT ISAAC TO PORT QUIN

DISTANCE/TIME	6 miles (9.7km) / 4hrs
ASCENT/GRADIENT	984ft (300m) / ▲ ▲ ▲
PATHS	Good coastal and field paths; strenuous steps on coast path and unfenced cliff edges; not suitable for small children; several stiles
LANDSCAPE	Coastal scenery and inland fields, one wooded valley
SUGGESTED MAP	OS Explorer 106 Newquay & Padstow
START/FINISH	Grid reference: SW999809
DOG FRIENDLINESS	Dogs on lead in fields and on coast path
PARKING	Port Isaac. Large car park on Port Gaverne side, busy in summer; another on B3267 on outskirts of village. Small car park at Port Quin
PUBLIC TOILETS	Port Isaac and at start of Roscarrock Hill

The north Cornish coast between the sea inlets of Port Isaac and Port Quin is a puzzle of tumbled cliffs and convoluted hills. The price is a strenuous coastal walk between the two. You rise and fall like a dipping gull, but without the same ease. The inland return across fields, to Port Isaac, is undramatic but not strenuous. On the coastal section, be prepared for airy clifftop paths that in places are pinned narrowly between thin air on the unprotected seaward edge and a lengthy stretch of wooden fencing inland, said by some ironic locals to be as visible from space as the Great Wall of China.

The North Cornwall village of Port Isaac is one of the county's most popular visitor destinations, even more so since the success of the ITV drama *Doc Martin*, which is filmed there. Part of the village's appeal also lies in its relative freedom from too many visitors' vehicles. The village is enclosed between the steep slopes of a narrow valley that reaches the sea at a protected inlet, a natural haven for vessels. It is this orientation to the sea that has produced the densely compact nature of the village. The sea was the common highway here, long before the modern road became so; until the early 20th century trading ships brought coal, limestone, timber and other commodities to Port Isaac and carried away fish, farm produce, mineral ore and building stone.

It's worth taking a little time to explore the village of Port Isaac (see While you're there) before setting off uphill on the coastal footpath. The path leads round the smooth-browed Lobber Point, then traces a remarkable rollercoaster route along the folded coastline to Kellan Head and then to Port Quin. There is a slightly haunted air about Port Quin today. It is a remote, silent place, yet in 1841 nearly 100 people lived here in a village of over 20 households. Now only a few cottages remain, not all of them occupied permanently. Like most inlets on the north Cornish coast Port Quin survived until the 19th century on pilchard fishing and on coastal trade that involved the import of coal and lime in exchange for slate and lead from small mining concerns. Legend claims that most of the men of Port Quin were lost at sea in some kind of fishing or smuggling disaster, and that the womenfolk and children moved away. There was certainly rapid depopulation, but it may simply have been through emigration when mining failed and pilchard fishing declined in the late 19th century. The route you follow through the fields back to bustling Port Isaac must once have been a local highway between two thriving communities.

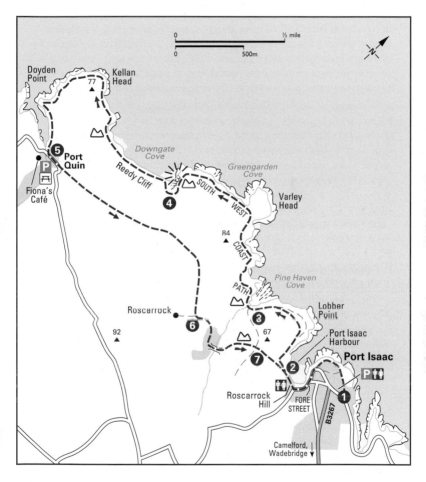

1. Leave Port Isaac's main car park by the lowest terrace and turn left along a surfaced track, keeping right where it branches, signposted 'Coast Path'. At the road, keep ahead and down Fore Street to reach the open space known as the Platt at the entry to the harbour. Just past Port Isaac Fishermen Ltd, turn right up Roscarrock Hill, signposted 'Coast Path'.

2. At the top of the lane, pass a public footpath sign on the left, then, in 30yds (27m), keep to the right of the gateway to a terrace of houses and bear right at a coast path acorn. Follow the path round Lobber Point.

3. Descend to Pine Haven Cove and then go through a kissing gate. (A wooden fence marches alongside the inside edge of the path from here on.) Climb steeply uphill and round the edge of an enormous gulf. Go through a kissing gate at the end of the fenced section and cross Varley Head to another kissing gate. The path ahead again runs close to the cliff edge and is fenced on the inside.

4. Just beyond a bench descend steep steps (there is a hand rail for a perilous section at the top) into Downgate Cove and Reedy Cliff. Follow the coast path up some very steep sections to reach the seaward edge of Kellan Head. Continue along the coast path until you reach Port Quin.

5. Turn left at Port Quin and go up the road past the car park entrance. At a bend in the road bear off left, to pass in front of Howard's Cottage. Keep up the slope to a metal gate beside a stone stile. Dogs should be kept under strict control from here on. Follow the path alongside a hedge, then climb to a stile between two gates. Keep alongside the right-hand edge of the next fields.

6. Go through an open gateway near Roscarrock (right), then turn left and follow the left field-edge to a gap by a wooden stile. Go left and descend into the wooded valley bottom. Cross a wooden footbridge over a stream, then go over a stone stile. Keep ahead and climb very steeply through gorse to reach an open field slope. Keep ahead across the field (no apparent path), aiming to the left of a tall wooden pole up ahead.

7. Cross a stone stile and follow the left field-edge downhill beneath thorn trees to a junction with the lane at waypoint 2. Turn right and retrace your steps to Port Isaac and the car park.

Where to eat and drink

The Salt Pig (seasonal) in the car park at Port Quin is great for a light breakfast, lunch or snack at the halfway point; in Port Isaac there is a wide variety of eating options. The Slipway, Outlaw's and the Mote Bar are clustered round The Platt, and the nearby Golden Lion has outside seating overlooking the harbour. Takeaway fish and chips and pasties can be bought on Fore Street.

What to see

The tangled vegetation of the Reedy Cliff area makes an ideal habitat for small birds such as the stonechat. This is a typical passerine, or percher. The male bird is easily distinguished by its russet breast, white collar and dark head, while the female is a duller brown overall. The 'stonechat' name derives from the bird's distinctive chattering note that resembles a rapid tapping of stone on stone.

While you're there

Take the opportunity to explore Port Isaac. The alleyways of the village reach their most eccentric form in the narrowest of passageways, known as 'drangs', with splendid names such as 'Shuggie's Ope' and 'Squeeze-ee-Belly Alley', the latter speaking for itself. Where Fore Street, at its bottom end, bends sharply round to the harbour, keep ahead along a narrow alley to find these passageways.

AROUND PENTIRE
POINT AND THE RUMPS

DISTANCE/TIME	4 miles (6.4km) / 2hr 30min
ASCENT/GRADIENT	270ft (83m) / ▲▲
PATHS	Clearly identifiable and good underfoot; may be muddy after rain and in winter
LANDSCAPE	A rugged flat-topped headland of very high cliffs backed by typical coastal heathland and close-cropped grass
SUGGESTED MAP	OS Explorer 106 Newquay & Padstow
START/FINISH	Grid reference: SW940799
DOG FRIENDLINESS	Lead required in areas where livestock might graze
PARKING	National Trust car park just beyond Pentireglaze
PUBLIC TOILETS	New Polzeath

In Cornwall you are spoiled for choice when it comes to mighty headlands above the glittering sea. This walk takes you onto one of the mightiest, at Pentire on the northern arm of Padstow Bay, the great estuary of the River Camel. The headland is ringed by towering black cliffs that rise to over 300ft (91m) in height. Volcanic activity has resulted in characteristic formations of pillow lava – layers of smooth dark rock caused by bubbling masses of red hot lava being extruded beneath the sea. The complexity of the area's geology is reflected in the Old Lead Mine area, where cars now park. Here, lead and silver mining began during the Tudor period and lasted until the late 19th century.

Pentire's most northerly point is dominated by the Rumps, a rugged and sea-battered fist of land embellished with dramatic pinnacles and with an accompanying offshore island known as the Mouls. This was once the site of an Iron Age 'cliff castle' or 'promontory fort'. The corrugated folds of three earth ramparts, with accompanying ditches, lie across the narrowest part of the neck and extend down either side to the very edge of the cliffs. The outermost rampart has a stone-flanked entrance, which would have been closed off with a massive wooden gate when the site was occupied during the period from about the second century BC until the first century AD. Excavations were carried out here during the 1970s, and late Iron Age pottery was found. There are also traces of Iron Age round houses at the site. Rather than being a defensive site, this type of 'cliff castle' may have been a commercial and cultural centre of local Iron Age communities as they developed a more settled and stable society.

The coast path skirts Pentire Point, an outstanding viewpoint. There are sweeping panoramas across Padstow Bay and the estuary of the River Camel, where the notorious sand bank known as Doom Bar has wrecked many vessels. Swathes of pink-flowered thrift and white bladderwort cover the slopes in spring and summer. The air is full of bird life, if you keep your eyes peeled. Look out for the noisy little stonechat and the musical skylark. Raptors include the brown-backed kestrel, typically hovering above the grass as it searches for food. You may catch sight of a peregrine falcon – bigger than the kestrel and with distinctive grey and white markings. The peregrine rarely hovers and is often seen high in the sky, wheeling and turning and at times dropping like a stone as it swoops down the cliffs. If you are very lucky, you may catch a glimpse of the Cornish chough, recognised by its sleek black feathers and distinctive red beak and legs. The chough is beginning to re-colonise the Cornish cliffs after a long absence.

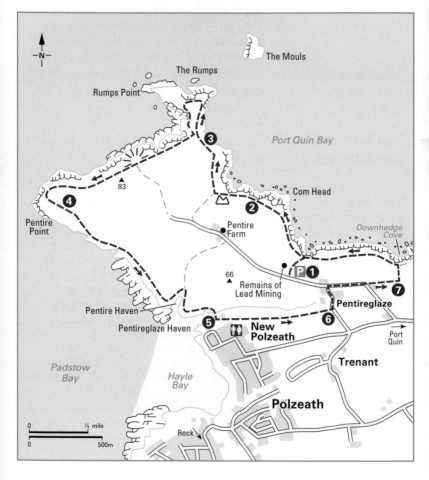

1. From the top corner of the car park take the footpath to the right of the National Trust map and information board. Soon cross a field and go through a gate to join the coastal footpath, signed 'Rumps'. Turn left along the Coast Path.

2. Go through a gate (dogs on lead here). Go up steps and continue steeply uphill and then downhill, and through another gate. Go through a gate and pass a side path to Pentire Farm. Reach a junction above the Rumps.

3. Take the right-hand branch downhill, and go through a gap in the wall to explore the Rumps. Returning from the Rumps, take the right-hand path from the gap in the wall and rejoin the Coast Path. Pass a signpost to Pentire Farm but keep to the Coast Path. Go through a gate and continue round Pentire Point, from where splendid views of Polzeath Beach and the Padstow Estuary open up.

4. Follow the Coast Path for the next mile (1.6km). Cross a small stream by the small sandy inlet of Pentire Haven. Ignore the path, signed 'Pentire Farm', that runs inland from this point. Follow the main path steeply uphill above the inlet of Pentireglaze Haven and then zig-zag downhill. Go through a gate and cross the head of the beach.

5. Turn left by houses at a T-junction with a track, and follow the track inland. Where the track bends sharply round to the right, keep straight ahead along a greenway. Go through a gate, signed 'National Trust Pentireglaze'. Keep straight ahead through fields and field gateways. Please keep dogs strictly under control here – cattle and sheep may be grazing.

6. Reach a surfaced lane and turn left to Pentireglaze Farm. At a T-junction turn right along a lane. (Note the board on the left displaying pictures of local wildlife.) Where the lane bends sharply right by a house, keep straight ahead along a farm track, signed 'To Coast Path'.

7. In 200yds (180m) turn sharply left down the edge of a field. Go through a kissing gate and turn left along the Coast Path above the rocky Downhedge Cove. Soon afterwards, pass through a kissing gate. Go through a gate and then turn immediately left through yet another gate. Head right across a small field to return to the car park.

Where to eat and drink

There are several cafés and restaurants in Polzeath. The Waterfront Bar and Grill offers a good range of sandwiches, pizzas, platters and lunch plates.

What to see

As always on such coastal headlands, the environment here seems entirely natural. Yet beside the car park you may notice several low hummocks. These are the surviving elements of an old lead mine that operated at various times from as early as the 16th century until late Victorian times.

While you're there

A mile or so to the east lies the hamlet of Port Quin. This was a busy settlement in previous centuries, when fishing boats and trading vessels anchored in the sheltered inlet. Until the mid-19th century up to 100 people lived at Port Quin. The dramatic depopulation has been explained as perhaps being caused by a disaster at sea in which the men of the cove were lost, although economic decline of fishing and mining is the more likely reason.

THROUGH CARDINHAM WOODS

DISTANCE/TIME	5.5 miles (8.8km) / 3hrs
ASCENT/GRADIENT	328ft (100m) / ▲
PATHS	Generally clear woodland tracks and field sections, several stiles
LANDSCAPE	Deep woodland of deciduous and conifer trees, quiet meadows
SUGGESTED MAP	OS Explorer 109 Bodmin Moor
START/FINISH	Grid reference: SX099666
DOG FRIENDLINESS	Dogs on lead through fields and under control in Cardinham Woods (no fouling of picnic areas, dog bins in car park)
PARKING	Cardinham Woods car park
PUBLIC TOILETS	At car park

Cardinham Woods lie east of Bodmin town, in the serene countryside drained by Cardinham Water and its tributaries. The 650 acres (263ha) that make up the combined Deviock, Hurtstocks, Callywith and Tawnamoor Woods of Cardinham have been in the hands of the Forestry Commission since 1922. The original woodland was used for a number of traditional rural industries, including charcoal burning. Some of the old woodland of oak, beech, hazel, birch and holly survives. The commercial timber includes larch, Sitka spruce and Douglas fir. Most of the tracks and paths throughout the woods are courtesy of the woodland management, and walkers must always heed notices indicating where work is being carried out.

There are a number of waymarked walking and cycling trails throughout the woods, but this walk takes you beyond to the hamlet of Cardinham and its handsome Church of St Meubred's. From the parking and picnic area at the entrance to Cardinham Woods the way leads along a broad forestry track above Cardinham Water to a major junction of tracks at Lady Vale Bridge. You turn immediately left before the bridge, but before doing so walk on a few paces and look at the little granite 'clapper' bridge that crosses the rushing stream down on the right. Now blocked off, this was known as Valebridge and was a major crossing point for centuries. Within the tangle of woodland behind the bridge is the site of Lady Vale Chapel, an early Christian site.

As you climb higher into the woods, the route leaves the managed forest and passes through the upper reaches of Lidcutt Wood, a witchlike world of old beech trees whose moss-covered trunks are entwined with thick columns of ivy that will send a shiver up your spine, if not your legs. Beyond here a quiet lane descends steeply to a field path that leads up to the Church of St Meubred (see While you're there). From the church you head back towards Cardinham Woods through old meadows and along ancient tracks that once served as a pilgrims' way to Lady Vale Chapel.

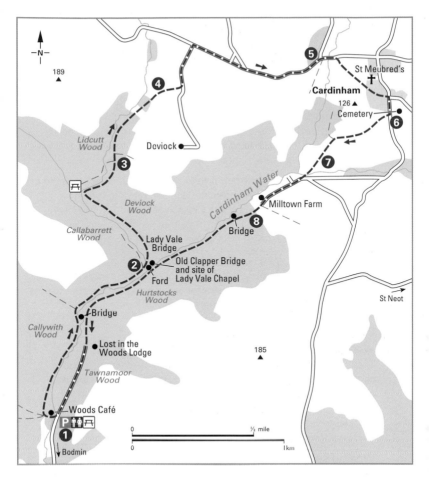

1. From the Cardinham Woods car park, cross the wooden bridge over Cardinham Water and pass the café and play area. Bear right, then right again through a wooden barrier to a three-way junction. Keep to the right and follow a broad forestry track through the woods with Cardinham Water to your right. Ignore a sign left to the Liddicoat Valley Walk.

2. Where a track comes in from the left, bear slightly right to cross a tributary stream (just before Lady Vale Bridge) and turn left up a track marked by a guide post that mentions various woodland walks. Soon you'll pass picnic tables by a little rock face on a bend.

3. Just before a bridge turn off right at a junction. In a few paces, ignore a turning right for the Bodmin Beast bike trail and keep straight ahead along a grassy track through Lidcutt Wood. Go over a stile and on through woods.

4. Emerge into a field and bear half right; the right of way heads straight across the field aiming for a wooden gate onto a concrete track. Turn left and follow the track to a public road. Turn right along the road and follow it over the brow of the hill and down into the valley.

5. Pass a lane junction and keep ahead downhill to cross a river, then go off right at a public footpath sign. Go over a stile and cross a little ditch. Head diagonally up the field, aiming to the right of Cardinham church tower, to cross a stile. Go along a grassy ride beside the church. Turn right at the road.

6. At a public footpath sign opposite a cemetery, go right and through a gate into a field. Aim for a guidepost in the middle of the field and carry on, following a faint track, keeping to the left of a tree. Go through two metal gates and keep alongside the hedge on the right. At a stile, where the track bends round right, bear off left and head downhill between trees to cross a meadow to a stile. This is the line of the right of way.

7. Bear diagonally left across the next field to a wooden gate. Keep ahead to a bridge over a stream, then follow a path through the trees. Go through a wooden gate and reach a T-junction with a lane at Milltown. Turn right here, down the lane and keep left at a junction. Pass Milltown Farm, and keep ahead to reach a wooden barrier. Go up a slope, then turn right at a junction with a forestry track.

8. Follow the track to reach the junction at Lady Vale Bridge, beside which the Old Clapper Bridge still stands. Keep straight ahead alongside the river to pass Lost in the Woods Lodge and return to the car park.

Where to eat and drink

There is a delightful riverside café, Woods, by the Cardinham Woods car park, in an old stonebuilt cottage, serving morning coffee, lunches and afternoon tea. You will find a range of food outlets in Bodmin 4 miles (6.5km) away, but if you want an authentic country pub, try The London Inn at St Neot, 8 miles (12.8km) to the east of Cardinham Woods.

What to see

If you are very lucky – and very quiet – you may spot the elusive roe deer. This is a small, handsome little deer with red-brown summer coat and long grey winter coat. The small antlers are very upright and usually have only three points.

While you're there

St Meubred's Church at Cardinham village is a handsome building both inside and out. The churchyard boasts two splendid Cornish crosses, one of which is well over 8ft (2m) high. The aisles have very fine wagon roofs, some parts of which retain original colouring, and these are more than matched by the 15th- to 16th-century pew ends. During World War II, St Meubred's was damaged by a bomb that was meant for Plymouth. It landed in the churchyard and destroyed the chancel windows.

THE RIVER CAMEL AT WADEBRIDGE

DISTANCE/TIME	6.5 miles (10.4km) / 3hrs
ASCENT/GRADIENT	328ft (100m) / ▲
PATHS	Farm tracks (sometimes muddy) and good forestry tracks; cycle path along old railway line
LANDSCAPE	Wooded riverside
SUGGESTED MAP	OS Explorer 106 Newquay & Padstow
START/FINISH	Grid reference: SW991722
DOG FRIENDLINESS	Dogs should be kept under control and restrained from roaming fields and property adjacent to the Camel Trail. On lead through grazed areas and if notices indicate
PARKING	Several car parks in Wadebridge
PUBLIC TOILETS	The Platt, Wadebridge

Wadebridge is emphatically a river town. Even its name defines it as such. Before the mid-15th century the settlement on the banks of the Camel River, upstream from Padstow, was known simply as 'Waed' – the fording place. It was a dangerous passage across the Camel here, and there were many drownings and close shaves. Eventually, in 1485, money was raised for the building of a bridge, known subsequently as 'The Bridge on Wool'. Contemporary records suggest that the foundations for the stone piers of the new bridge were actually made up of wool sacks. Another, less appealing but possibly more accurate, explanation is that the money for the bridge was earned from the lucrative wool trade of the medieval period. The bridge has 17 arches and is 320ft (98m) long. It was widened in 1847 and is recognised as being one of the finest examples of a medieval bridge in Britain.

In the 19th century Wadebridge also acquired a famous railway, first linking the town to Bodmin in 1875 and then to Padstow in 1899. The Wadebridge to Bodmin section was built to carry sand extracted from the Camel Estuary for agricultural use to improve soil conditions. In return the railway carried china clay and granite from the quarries on Bodmin Moor for export by sea. Extending the railway line to Padstow led to the decline of Wadebridge as a port, but the Padstow link also established the line as part of the great Atlantic Coast Express, carrying huge numbers of holidaymakers from London and the heart of England to the Cornish seaside resorts. The journey from Bodmin through Wadebridge to Padstow was immortalised by the poet John Betjeman, who described it as 'the most beautiful train journey...'

The line was closed in the 1960s. In 1980 Cornwall County Council bought the section from Boscarne Junction near Bodmin to Padstow and turned it into a recreational trail, the Camel Trail, that has subsequently been enjoyed by vast numbers of walkers, cyclists, horse riders, anglers and birders. This walk follows part of the Camel Trail, but first leads inland through deeply wooded countryside. The route climbs steadily to the serene hamlet of Burlawn before it descends into an enfolding blanket of woodland by Hustyn Mill. From here it leads to Polbrock Bridge, where the River Camel and the Camel Trail cling to each other like enamoured snakes. From Polbrock Bridge you follow the Camel Trail effortlessly back to Wadebridge, in more crowded circumstances at times and sharing the experience with cyclists, yet within that same persuasive world of trees, river and Cornish air that so enchanted Betjeman.

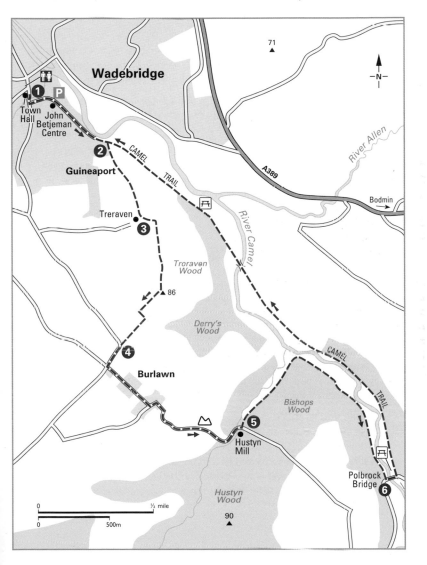

1. The walk starts on The Platt in the centre of Wadebridge. Face the town hall and turn left. Cross Trecuddick Bridge and turn left on Trevanion Road. Pass the John Betjeman Centre and continue along the Guineaport Road, following the Camel Trail.

2. At the fork, keep right (leaving the Camel Trail) and within a few paces, at a junction where the road curves up to the right, keep ahead along an unsurfaced track signposted 'Public footpath Treraven 1/3m'. Follow the track steadily uphill. Go through a wooden gate and follow the right-hand field-edge to go through another gate. Continue along a track to reach a junction in front of Treraven farm.

3. Go left and follow the track as it bears right to a junction. Turn right, soon following the track to the left, and continue along the track to reach a bend on a minor public road by a house.

4. Keep straight ahead along the road, with care, then turn left at a crossroads, signed 'Burlawn'. At the next junction bear left and follow the road through Burlawn. Go steeply downhill on a narrow lane overshadowed by trees.

5. At Hustyn Mill, beyond a little footbridge and a public footpath, turn left off the road past a barrier and follow a broad woodland track through Bishops Wood. Stay on the main track to where it reaches the surfaced road at Polbrock Bridge.

6. Turn left over the bridge across the River Camel and, in a few paces, go off left and down steps to join the Camel Trail. Turn left here and follow the unwavering line of the Camel Trail back to Wadebridge.

Where to eat and drink

There are no refreshment outlets along the route, but Wadebridge has a number of pubs, restaurants and cafés. The Swan Hotel on the corner of The Platt and Molesworth Street, the town's main street leading to its famous bridge, does good traditional food.

What to see

The River Camel and its flanking woods are a perfect habitat for birds. Look for goldfinch and nuthatch among the trees, and for heron and curlew on the river. In the spring and autumn, if you are very lucky, you may spot birds of passage such as the beautiful little egret in its snow-white plumage.

While you're there

Visit the John Betjeman Centre in Southern Way, Wadebridge. It's in the old railway station and contains memorabilia of the famous Poet Laureate. He was unsurpassed as a chronicler of suburbia and the countryside, and a lover of the Padstow and Wadebridge area where he had a family home. Refreshments are available at the centre.

PADSTOW AND THE CAMEL ESTUARY

DISTANCE/TIME	3.5 miles (5.6km) / 2hrs
ASCENT/GRADIENT	197ft (60m) / ▲
PATHS	Surfaced walkways, coastal footpath and country lane, several stiles
LANDSCAPE	Traditional fishing village and estuary shoreline
SUGGESTED MAP	OS Explorer 106 Newquay & Padstow
START/FINISH	Grid reference: SW917753
DOG FRIENDLINESS	Dogs on lead through grazed areas. Dogs on lead welcomed in the grounds of Prideaux Place
PARKING	Padstow main car park on outskirts of town; car park at Padstow Harbour and old railway station
PUBLIC TOILETS	Main car park; The Strand (ladies only), Padstow Harbour

The popular north Cornish port of Padstow is a delightful town, particularly famous for its May Day festival of the 'Obby Oss', during which symbolic hobby horses, made of great hooped masks with trailing black skirts, are danced round the streets in celebration of ancient fertility rites. It is a truly unforgettable and slightly eerie experience, but well worth attending.

Attempting a quiet stroll here has become increasingly difficult since chef Rick Stein 'set up shop' In Padstow in the mid-1970s. Visitors flock here in their thousands to walk the narrow streets and soak up the sun on the harbourside, their numbers swelled further by those arriving by bicycle on the Camel Trail from Wadebridge and beyond along the former line of the North Cornwall Railway. But it is possible to escape the hordes by taking the coast path alongside the Camel Estuary towards Stepper Point; the views across the estuary to Brea Hill (Sir John Betjeman is buried at St Enodoc Church, in sand dunes beyond), Daymer Bay and, in the distance, Pentire Point, are stunning.

Padstow's history stretches back to Celtic times when the missionary St Petroc, son of a Welsh prince, founded a monastery here in AD 600. There are no remains of the monastery, but the 15th-century Church of St Petroc, visited on the route, is dedicated to the saint. A substantial building, the church has a broad nave and aisles and fine wagon roofs and artefacts, including a splendid font in Cataclews stone from Cataclews Point at nearby Harlyn Bay. The church marks the northern end of the 30-mile (48km) Saints Way, a walking route which crosses the county to St Fimbarrus Church in Fowey.

During the 17th century Padstow was home to a thriving shipbuilding industry, and the town still has an active fishing fleet. Many of the quaint old fishermen's cottages now house holidaymakers, galleries, craft shops and cafés. After an exploration of the town, the walk goes along the estuary, before a return through fields and lanes to reach Prideaux Place in time for tea.

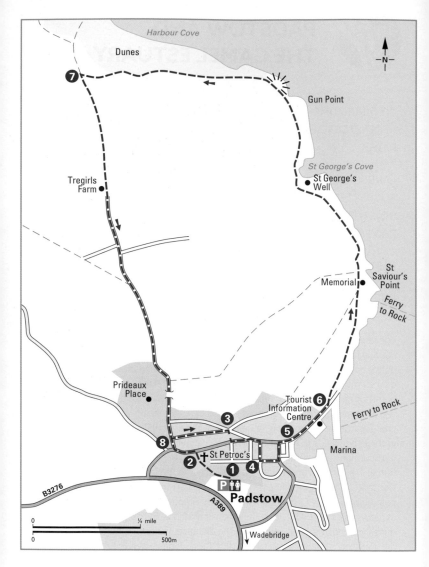

1. From the town's main car park, leave from the bottom right-hand corner, to the left of the toilets, signed 'Town Centre'. At a junction with a walkway turn left. (From the lower car park, leave by steps at the bottom and turn left.) Follow the walkway to the churchyard of St Petroc's Church. Facing the porch, turn left, then walk through the churchyard between tall yews. Go through an ornate metal kissing gate into Church Street, opposite Poppy Cottage.

2. Turn left up to a junction with Tregirls Lane. Turn right and almost immediately right again into the High Street. The houses and buildings in this part of Padstow feature some of the town's finest vernacular architecture.

3. Just before the High Street's junction with Cross Street, go right through a fascinating passageway, Marble Arch. Watch your head at low sections and

reach steps that lead into Church Street once more. Turn left and join Duke Street at a junction with Cross Street. Bear right and walk down the raised terrace of Duke Street; where that ends go right along Middle Street.

4. At the end of Middle Street, turn into Lanadwell Street, passing the Golden Lion Hotel and the London Inn. At the end of Lanadwell Street reach Broad Street. Turn left here and walk along the busy Market Place, then on down an alleyway past the Old Ship Hotel, to emerge at The Strand and the harbour.

5. Turn left and walk along the harbour's North Quay past Abbey House, a distinctive slate-hung medieval building, with an open mullion window, below which is a stone head in a niche. Continue to where the road forks, just past the Shipwrights pub and the Tourist Information Centre.

6. Keep left here uphill, signposted 'Coast Path' and 'To Lower Beach'. Follow the walkway through Chapel Stile Field and on to a war memorial at St Saviour's Point, then follow the coast path past St George's Cove and Gun Point. Continue along the path above sand dunes to reach a stile into a field. Follow the field-edge, cross another stile, and reach a T-junction with a stony track.

7. Turn left and uphill to Tregirls Farm (holiday cottages). Go through the gateway to your right and continue heading uphill. Follow the surfaced lane from the farm for about 0.33 miles (536m), then pass beneath an archway and reach the Elizabethan building of Prideaux Place (see While you're there). Continue to the end of Tregirls Lane.

8. Turn left down Church Street. Opposite Poppy Cottage go through the churchyard gate and retrace your steps to the car park. Alternatively continue down Church Street and back to reach Padstow Harbour.

Where to eat and drink
Rick Stein has a number of establishments in the town; these are matched by other fine restaurants and a host of food outlets, as well as pubs and traditional inns. Excellent pasties are made at the Chough Bakery on the Harbour; Prideaux Place has the Terrace Tearoom.

What to see
Along the banks of the Camel Estuary, at Gun Point and above the dunes, look for maritime plants such as early scurvy grass, with glossy leaves and pink flowers, the red-tinged sea beet and sea rocket, a straggling plant with green fleshy leaves and pale lilac flowers. Look for coltsfoot too, with its yellow daisy-like head and a silvery stem.

While you're there
At the end of the described route is Prideaux Place, an Elizabethan house that has been lived in by the Prideaux-Brune family for over 400 years. There are guided tours of the house and its sumptuously furnished rooms, and the landscaped gardens are also open to the public. The house is open at Easter and from early May to late October.

TREVONE AND GUNVER HEAD

DISTANCE/TIME	2.5 miles (4km) / 1hr 30min
ASCENT/GRADIENT	196ft (60m) / ▲
PATHS	Farm tracks and easy cliff-top paths (take care near cliff edges), several stiles
LANDSCAPE	A coastline of fascinating rock formations and unique geology
SUGGESTED MAP	OS Explorer 106 Newquay & Padstow
START/FINISH	Grid reference: SW892759
DOG FRIENDLINESS	Lead required in field sections and on open cliff-tops where cattle may be grazing
PARKING	Trevone Beach
PUBLIC TOILETS	None on route

Go for a walk at Gunver Head and you'll see spectacular geology at every turn. Cornwall is at the cutting edge of coastal geology in more ways than one. The county's coastline is where erosion by sea and weather and by simple gravity holds sway. Together these forces of nature have exposed the geological lie of the land to show us what the ground beneath our feet is made of.

The walk starts at Trevone Bay, one of those lovely punctuation marks in North Cornwall's otherwise endless wall of sea cliffs. Here, land and sea meet gently at a broad apron of tide-washed golden sand, ideal for all beach activities including surfing. The beach gets very busy at the height of summer, but is less popular in the quieter periods of the year. From the beach at Trevone the walk leads inland along lanes and farm tracks past the hamlet of Crugmeer. Beyond here the coast is reached at Gunver Head, where some serious geology begins. Giant pinnacles and tottering lumps of rock are made up of masses of shale shot through with myriad complexities – the end products of cataclysmic earth movements millions of years ago. What we see, in fact, are the wasted and eroded roots of mountains that were formed during vast earth movements that took place long before humans walked on earth. These fantastic giant chess pieces are easily viewed from the cliff path.

The Meropes are a sequence of offshore islands and rocky stacks that lie a mere stone's throw from the mainland beyond a narrow rocky channel known as Tregudda Gorge. The most distinctive of the stacks is Middle Merope, a slender offshore tower of earth and rock that culminates in a narrow flat-topped pinnacle. Further south is the feature known as Porthmissen Bridge, a huge grass-topped bulwark which is linked to the mainland by a very narrow ridge of rock, earth and grass and is pierced by an archway at sea level. Further south again is the Marble Cliff on which more than 140 parallel bands of shale and limestone create a fascinating pattern. However, the area's remarkable geology is not finished yet. Keep to the cliff-edge path that leads back towards Trevone and you'll reach Roundhole Point, a sunny little headland of tan-coloured dolerite rock. Just a few yards inland from the point is the spectacular Round Hole, a huge circular pit more than 80ft (25m) deep, caused by the sea effectively tunnelling into the base of the cliff and undermining the soft ground above until it collapsed.

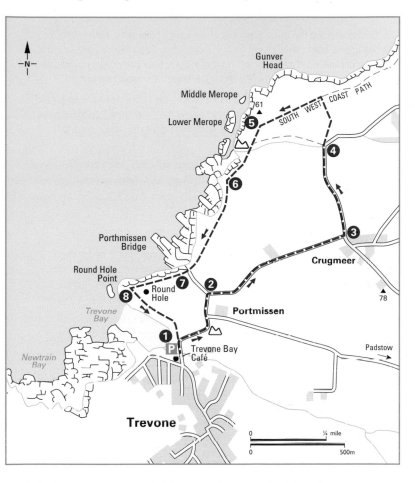

1. Go down steps at the end of the car park, to the left of the café entrance. Turn left and follow a lane that bends right above the beach. Keep to this lane as it rises uphill.

2. Stay on the lane where it levels off at a junction with a track to the left. Go through a gap and continue along the surfaced lane through open fields to the little hamlet of Crugmeer.

3. Turn left at Crugmeer and follow a narrow lane towards the coast. Follow the road round to the right, to a small parking area.

4. Pass another small parking area in about 30yds (27m) and in a few paces go left down a short overgrown path, and cross a wooden stile into a field. (If the footpath is impassable, head back 30yds (27m), go through a kissing gate and bear half right along a grassy track to the field wall, where you'll join the route

again.) Follow the right-hand edge of the field to reach a junction with the coast path. Turn left and follow the coast path round Gunver Head.

5. Follow the path steeply downhill into the bottom of a narrow valley, cross a stile and a stream, and continue less steeply uphill. There are dramatic views back to Lower Merope Island and Middle Merope.

6. Continue along the coast path and cross a high slate stile. Now follow a broad grassy track, well inland from the cliff edge. Soon reach a gravelly track, and several paces ahead bear off right along a grassy path. Skirt round some herringbone-patterned walls. Porthmissen Bridge is visible to the right.

7. Keep to the right and follow the coast path to the rocky headland of Round Hole Point, where there are picnic spots below the path. Just inland from the Point is the famous Round Hole. Take great care if looking down from the edges of the hole.

8. Continue along the coast path. Cross a stone stile and reach concrete steps leading down to the lane at Trevone Beach. Turn right, cross above the beach and return to the car park.

Where to eat and drink

Trevone Bay Café is beside the car park at Trevone Beach and serves breakfast, light lunches, cream teas and snacks as well as hot and cold drinks. They also have a takeaway pizza service. On the walk there are several good picnic spots.

What to see

The sea stacks and crumbling cliffs around Gunver Head and the Meropes offer ideal habitats for seabirds. Common gulls are always around, but during spring and summer look out for razorbills and guillemots, both similar in having black backs and white 'apron' fronts. Their bills are the key to identification: the razorbill has a short, thick, blunt beak with a thin white vertical band, while the guillemot has a longer, thinner beak and a smaller head.

While you're there

Enjoy a swim from Trevone Beach. The beach is greatly reduced at high tide. You should always pay attention to the lifeguards, who are on duty from mid-May until the end of September. A dog ban operates at the beach from Easter until the end of September.

EXPLORING BEDRUTHAN STEPS AND PARK HEAD

DISTANCE/TIME	4.5 miles (7.2km) / 2hrs 30min
ASCENT/GRADIENT	131ft (40m) / ▲ ▲
PATHS	Coastal paths and field paths. Coast path very close to unguarded cliff edges in some places; take care in windy weather and with children and dogs
LANDSCAPE	Spectacular cliffs and dramatic sea stacks
SUGGESTED MAP	OS Explorer 106 Newquay & Padstow
START/FINISH	Grid reference: SW850691
DOG FRIENDLINESS	Dogs on lead through grazed areas
PARKING	National Trust car park at Carnewas; or at the National Trust Park Head car park
PUBLIC TOILETS	Carnewas car park

The flat, unremarkable countryside that lies inland from Bedruthan Steps belies the stupendous nature of the area's coastline. Green fields run to the sliced-off edges of 300ft (90m) cliffs. At the foot of the cliffs lie dramatic rock islands that at high tide are besieged by crashing waves and at low tide spring from a smooth expanse of golden, sea-damp sand. This was Victorian 'picturesque' at its most melodramatic, and the area was popular with 'excursionists' in the late 19th century. The islands, or stacks, are portrayed as being the stepping stones of a legendary giant called Bedruthan, but this conceit blew in with the first of the Victorian tourists. The stacks acquired picturesque names such as 'The Queen Bess Rock', which, before losing its head to erosion, was said to resemble the figure of Elizabeth I, who never lost her head in any sense.

For many years, before tourists and tall tales of giants, there were flights of steps cut into the cliff faces below Carnewas and further north at Pentire in the crook of coastline south of Park Head. These staircases were known as Carnewas Steps and Pentire Steps, and were probably used by local people to collect seaweed and to land cargoes, legitimate or otherwise. During the 19th century, when the mines at Carnewas were in use, the miners may also have sought access to the beach as the tin, copper and lead may have originally been extracted from tunnels, known as adits, at the base of the cliffs. (The National Trust shop and tea room are housed in old mine buildings.)

Today you can reach Bedruthan Beach down a secure staircase from the coast path, partway along the route of the walk from the start at Carnewas car park (see While you're there). From the top of the steps the coast path leads north towards Park Head passing, on the way, the vestigial remains of Redcliff Castle, an Iron Age fortified settlement whose landward embankments are all that remain of a protruding headland long since collapsed into the sea. From beyond Redcliff Castle, one of the finest views of Bedruthan Beach can be had;

do not go too close to the cliff edge. The circuit of Park Head, via the pleasant cove of Porth Mear, rounds off the walk. You can walk out to the promontory of Park Head itself, passing through the defensive banks of another Iron Age fortified settlement across the neck of the headland. From here the coast path leads back past Redcliff Castle and then on towards Carnewas.

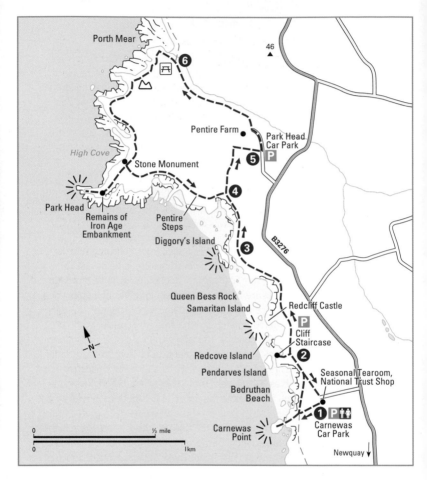

1. From Carnewas car park, go through a gap in the wall on the right of the National Trust shop, then, in a few paces, bear off to the left at a junction. Follow the path, keeping left to a crossing of paths beyond a gap in a low embankment, and go straight across and down a grassy path for the dramatic view from Carnewas Point of Bedruthan Beach and the sea stacks. Return to the crossing and follow a path left along the cliff edge. (Take heed of warning notices.) At a junction with a cobbled path, go left and descend to a dip at Pendarves Point.

2. At a junction in the dip, go down left to reach the top of the cliff staircase. On re-ascending the staircase, avoid the badly eroded path on the immediate left. Instead go back uphill to the junction with the coast path and turn left past a

National Trust sign, alongside a wooden fence, below a parking area, and then past the overgrown embankments of Redcliff Castle.

3. Where the path forks by a National Trust signpost marked 'Park Head', follow either fork to where they rejoin. Keep to the right of a stone wall that has tamarisk trees sprouting from it, to reach a wooden kissing gate. Continue along the open cliff top to reach a set of wooden gates on the right.

4. Go right through the kissing gate, then follow a permissive footpath along field-edges. Just before the buildings at Pentire, go right through a gate and follow field-edges to Park Head car park.

5. Turn immediately left and go down a surfaced lane. Just before the Pentire farm buildings go through a gate on the right, signposted 'Porth Mear Beach and Park Head'. Bear left across the field to a stile and gateway. Bear right down the next field to a wooden kissing gate in its bottom corner. Go through the gate and follow a path through a wetland area to join the coast path above the attractive Porth Mear.

6. Keep left and follow the coast path steadily uphill through a kissing gate and then round Park Head. Take care when close to the cliff edges. At a stone monument above High Cove, divert right to the promontory of Park Head itself. Return to the plaque and follow the coast path south to waypoint 4. Retrace your steps to waypoint 2, in the dip above the start of the cliff staircase. Follow the cobbled walkway uphill and back to Carnewas car park.

Where to eat and drink

There aren't any refreshment opportunities on the route, but there are National Trust tea rooms at Carnewas car park, open in summer.

What to see

At low water on the beach watch out for turnstones, brisk little birds with chestnut and black and white plumage and small heads. They dash across the damp sand 'turning' over stones in search of tiny shellfish and sandhoppers. Along the tops of the cliffs watch also for the silent, unflappable flight of the stubby-winged fulmar. This remarkable seabird was once found only in far northern waters and is believed to have spread south by following herring fishing boats returning to their English ports.

While you're there

A descent of the cliff staircase to Bedruthan Beach should not be missed, if you feel fit enough. The steps have been ably secured by the National Trust and are protected from the risk of falling stones by vast swathes of wire netting. Be careful on the rocky foreshore, where the rock can be very slippery. At low tide you can explore the beach, but be very aware of tide times, the flooding tide can cut you off very quickly. The day's tide times are usually displayed at the top of the steps. You are not advised to swim from Bedruthan Beach. The staircase is closed to the public from November to February.

ALONG THE COAST TO PERRANPORTH

DISTANCE/TIME	8 miles (12.9km) / 4hrs
ASCENT/GRADIENT	492ft (150m) / ▲
PATHS	Good coastal footpath and firm sandy beaches, several stiles
LANDSCAPE	Big sandy beaches and grassy cliff tops
SUGGESTED MAP	OS Explorer 104 Redruth & St Agnes
START/FINISH	Grid reference: SW788608
DOG FRIENDLINESS	Dogs on leads through grazed areas
PARKING	Crantock Beach (National Trust), Perranporth Beach car park
PUBLIC TOILETS	Crantock village; Crantock Beach car park; Perranporth
NOTES	Park early at Perranporth and catch the bus to Crantock to start rather than getting a bus at the end of the walk

West of Newquay the Cornish coast takes a turn for the dramatic. A series of broad, sandy beaches – some of the best in Cornwall – open between windswept headlands offering epic prospects: this is a surfers' shore. Holywell Bay and Perranporth offer some of Europe's best wave-riding conditions, and surfers from across Britain and beyond flock here year-round. Visitors have been battling the waves of this coast for centuries. According to legend, St Piran, the patron saint of tin miners and the best known of the so-called 'Celtic Saints' who brought Christianity to Cornwall in the 6th century, came ashore through the surf at Perranporth ('Piran's Beach' in Cornish) after crossing from Ireland on a miraculously buoyant millstone. The remains of St Piran's Oratory lie in the deep dunes of Penhale.

The walk begins in the car park at Crantock, a genteel village with a beach, popular with families. This spot is just a stone's throw from the brash bustle of Newquay, Cornwall's biggest resort. But the Gannel, a narrow estuary at the northern edge of Crantock Beach, cuts off the world of bars and surf-shops from the wilder shores to the west. From Crantock, the route follows the meandering course of the South West Coast Path to the sheltered inlet of Porth Joke, known locally as Polly Joke. From Porth Joke the route crosses the broad, rabbit-cropped back of Kelsey Head, and descends to Holywell Bay with its wide beach backed by sand dunes. The bay is named for a sacred spring, set in a cave in the cliffs. As recently as the 19th century pilgrims from across Cornwall would visit the spot at low tide in search of cures for all manner of debilitating illnesses. Beyond Holywell the route skirts the edge of the Penhale army camp to Ligger Point, where a magnificent view of the coastline opens. Ahead lies the grand 3-mile (4.8km) strip of sand that leads all the way to journey's end in the bustling seaside streets of Perranporth.

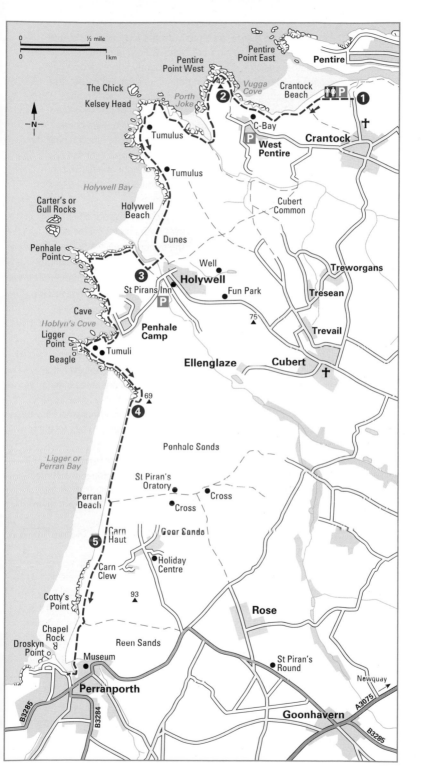

1. Follow the enclosed path that leads off to the left a few paces inside the entrance to the National Trust car park at Crantock. Fork left and follow a footworn grassy path across the dunes, bearing slightly left towards a half-hidden modern house with an hexagonal outbuilding. Near the house, first pass a junction with a path going right, then immediately reach another junction by a sign for 'The Rushy Green'. Keep right here (if you start from the centre of Crantock village, you should head down Beach Road, then immediately turn off left along a track which leads you to the junction near the house, at which you turn right). In a few paces reach a crossing of sandy tracks. Go straight ahead into an open field, then turn right and follow the field-edge. Keep ahead past the end of the beach where several paths branch inland to the left, including one to C-Bay, a café and bar.

2. After a kissing gate, bear left at a junction, and continue around Pentire Point West to Porth Joke. Cross the head of the beach and follow the coast path to Holywell Bay. Follow a path through the dunes to reach a bridge over a stream (you can divert inland here to public toilets, shops and St Pirans Inn).

3. Cross the back of the beach and bear right to a slate coast path marker signed 'Holywell'. Follow the coast path steeply uphill, passing a sign warning of adders and a Ministry of Defence sign about the army training camp at Penhale. Where it levels off, bear up to the left to pass between a compound of metal aerials and a wired-off mine shaft. Continue alongside the perimeter of the army camp to Ligger Point where Perran Beach comes into view.

4. Go downhill along a wide, gravelly path to reach the top of the beach itself. At most times it is possible to walk along the beach from here at least as far as the cliffs at Carn Haut. However, during high spring tides it may be necessary to follow the network of paths through the dunes. These are not always easy to follow, but they are sporadically marked with coast path signs – keep heading generally parallel to the beach.

5. At low tide you can continue along the beach all the way to Perranporth. At high tide climb a concrete ramp beside a lifeguard hut to the top of the cliff at Carn Haut. Where steps lead up left, keep straight on to a turning area. Join the coast path beyond a crash barrier and then continue to Perranporth town.

Where to eat and drink
Early in the walk the coast path passes C-Bay, where you can enjoy morning coffee, lunch or afternoon tea. At Holywell Bay there's a café and the St Pirans Inn. In summer there are often small refreshment shacks on Holywell Beach and midway along Perran Beach. There are pubs and cafés at Crantock and Perranporth.

What to see
The sand dunes of this section of Cornish coast support a fascinating range of flowering plants that are specially adapted to survive in the salt-laden environment of the sea shore.

While you're there
The main attractions of this walk are the various beaches passed en route.

THROUGH BISHOP'S WOOD

DISTANCE/TIME	3.5 miles (5.7km) / 2hrs 30min
ASCENT/GRADIENT	164ft (50m) / ▲
PATHS	Forest tracks and paths. Can be very muddy after rain
LANDSCAPE	Mixed woodland
SUGGESTED MAP	OS Explorer 105 Falmouth & Mevagissey
START/FINISH	Grid reference: SW820477
DOG FRIENDLINESS	Dogs are welcome throughout the woods. The authorities ask that owners clear up their dogs' mess
PARKING	Forestry car park, north of Idless, near Truro
PUBLIC TOILETS	None on route
NOTES	Car park gates close at sunset. Working woodland; please take note of signs advising of work in progress

The woods in Cornwall are always a delightful antidote to the county's surfeit of sea. Bishop's Wood near Truro is a part of the much larger St Clement Woods, and acquired its name from the time it was owned by the Bishop of Exeter during the late medieval period. Long before this, when the ancient woodland of the area had already been stripped bare by the early farmers, the highest point of the wood was crowned by a fortified Iron Age settlement.

Today, the substantial banks of the settlement survive, muffled by dense woodland cover. In later centuries, when tree cover was re-established here, the area would have been a typical working woodland. The Iron Age site is densely covered with coppiced oaks, identifiable by multiple trunks at the base. When the woods were actively managed for coppicing, the trunks would be cut so that new growth started in several places at once. They would be allowed to grow like this for up to 20 years or so before being harvested for charcoal making, basket making or a host of other wood products. Up to the beginning of the 20th century many woods were managed in this way. The practice is beginning to be re-introduced in some areas in Cornwall, because of its beneficial effects on wildlife habitats.

The walk starts from the forestry car park at the south end of the woods and leads along its eastern edge through Lady's Wood, on a track that is wonderfully eerie and enclosed. A robust little stream runs below the track. Beech trees dominate here, and further into the wood oak, hazel, birch, Japanese larch and holly lie to either side of the track. In spring the trees are bright with fresh leaves and the rich earth beneath the trees supports a wealth of plants, ferns and mosses. Look particularly for wood sorrel, bluebells, three-cornered leeks and the feathery fronds of male ferns. The track leads on to the top end of the wood just before Lanner Mill. Here you turn uphill and on to a broad forestry road that leads back south along the higher ridge of the woods. Halfway along you can divert left from the track to visit the site of the Iron Age settlement. The large bank and ditch that encircled the site is still visible. The rigid upper branches of the numerous coppiced oak trees enclose the central trunks of the trees like cages. This is a well-preserved site, although the trees and scrub blur the impact of the large bank and ditch construction. Such hilltop sites date from between the Bronze and Iron Ages and reflect a growing territorialism.

These were not forts in the narrow sense of being built purely for defence. They were defensible sites, certainly, but they were commercial and cultural centres as much as anything else, being the focus of a large territory of scattered farmsteads and settlements from which the unforested hilltop site would be easily seen. The hilltop 'fort' or 'castle' represented a central refuge in times of trouble, but served also as a place to bring livestock to market and to exchange household goods and to socialise and celebrate. From the Iron Age site, the last part of the walk takes you on to even higher ground through mature conifers and then through deciduous woodland.

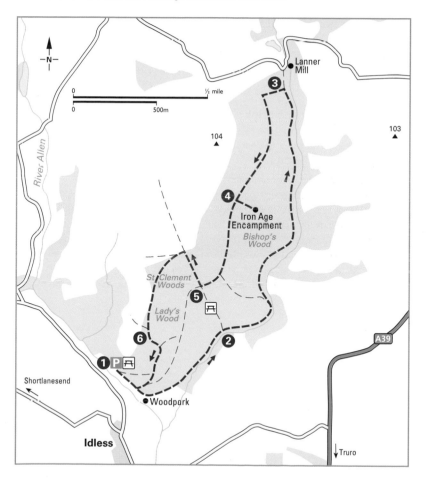

1. Leave the top end of the car park via the wooden barrier and go along a broad track. In a few paces, at a fork, keep to the right and follow the track above Woodpark and along the inside edge of the wood.

2. Keep ahead on the main track, walking parallel to the river, ignoring branch tracks leading off to the left. Keep ahead past the next three forks in the track.

3. Just at the northern end of the wood, with a glimpse of a tarmac road ahead, you reach a fork. Keep to the main track as it bends left and uphill. Keep left at a crossing which continues uphill and soon merges with a broad forestry road. Keep ahead along this road.

4. In about 0.4 miles (0.6km) look for three adjacent tracks on your left. These lead in about 20yds (18m) to the Iron Age fort, now very overgrown, but still discernible. Return back along the track to rejoin the main route.

5. At a bend beside a wooden bench, where tracks lead off to the left and right, go right by a signpost and follow a narrow trench-like track uphill between trees and follow a public footpath. At a path crossing turn left. Follow a rutted, muddy path/track through trees for about 0.4 miles (0.6km).

6. At a fork near the edge of the woods, bear sharp left. Soon bear right at the next fork to go steeply downhill. Shortly afterwards, reach another fork. Either way will take you to the car park just below but the right-hand path will guide you past picnic tables first.

Where to eat and drink

Woodman's Cabin, by the car park at Idless Wood, serves drinks, snacks and all-day breakfasts. There is also the Old Plough pub at Shortlanesend about 1 mile (1.6km) to the west of Idless.

What to see

Old woods are often rich in fungi. Look for the trunks of dead trees and you may find the great plate-like layers of various bracket fungi. Other fungi to look for among the rich humus of the woodland underlayer are stinkhorn fungus, the rudely unmistakable *Phallus impudicus*. On oak trees look for the round, woody growths called 'oak apples'. These are produced by gall wasps laying their eggs on oak leaves. The oak apple grows around the egg to protect it. Look closely and you may see a tiny hole where the adult insect has emerged.

AROUND REDRUTH

DISTANCE/TIME	4 miles (6.4km) / 2hrs 30 min
ASCENT/GRADIENT	442ft (135m) / ▲
PATHS	Field paths, rough tracks and surfaced lanes; may be muddy; several stiles
LANDSCAPE	Small fields and open heathland with quarry and mine remains
SUGGESTED MAP	OS Explorer 104 Redruth & St Agnes
START/FINISH	Grid reference: SW699421
DOG FRIENDLINESS	On a lead through grazed areas
PARKING	Several car parks in Redruth
PUBLIC TOILETS	Redruth car parks; Gwennap Pit Visitor Centre, when open

The old Cornish town of Redruth gained its name from mineral mining. In medieval times, the process of separating tin and copper from waste materials turned a local river blood-red with iron oxide. The Cornish name for a nearby ford was Rhyd Druth, the 'red ford', and the village that grew around it became Redruth. The innovative engineering that developed in tandem with mining turned Redruth and its adjoining town of Camborne into centres of Cornish industry and brought prosperity to the area, especially during the 19th century.

Into the often bleak world of 18th-century mineral mining came brothers John and Charles Wesley, burning with religious zeal; it's apt that one of the most revered locations in Methodism is Gwennap Pit, near Redruth. Here the grassy hollow of a caved-in mine shaft was first used for secular gatherings and events. However, it wasn't long before the pit was commandeered as a venue for preaching. John Wesley preached here between 1762 and 1789.

The first part of this walk leads from the heart of Redruth past such significant mining relics as the great chimney stack of the Pednandrea Mine, just off Sea View Terrace. Once the stack towered eight storeys high; it's now reduced to four, but is still impressive. From here you soon climb to the high ground of Gwennap and Carn Marth. The field path that takes you to Gwennap Pit was once a 'highway' of people heading to this 'cathedral of the moor'. Today there is a visitor centre at the Pit, alongside the peaceful little Busveal Chapel of 1836. From Gwennap Pit the walk leads on to the summit of Carn Marth and to one of the finest viewpoints in Cornwall; unexpectedly so because of the hill's modest profile. From above the flooded quarry on the summit you look north to the sea and to the hill of St Agnes Beacon. Northeast lies the St Austell clay country; southwest is the rocky summit of Carn Brea with its distinctive granite cross; southeast you can even see the cranes on Falmouth dockside. From the top of Carn Marth, the return route is all downhill along rough tracks and quiet country lanes that lead back to the heart of Redruth.

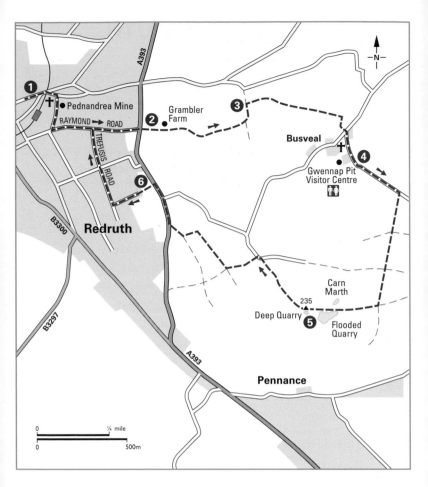

1. From any of the car parks, make your way to Fore Street, the main street of Redruth. Walk up to a junction (the railway station is down to the right) and take the middle branch, to the left of the Wesley Centenary Memorial Building and signposted 'To Victoria Park'. This is Wesley Street. In just a few paces turn right on Sea View Terrace; the chimney stack of the Pednandrea Mine (see While you're there) is up to the left a few paces along the road. Pass Basset Street on the right and, where streets cross, go left, all the way up Raymond Road to a T-junction with Sandy Lane.

2. Cross the road with care, then follow the track opposite, signposted 'Public Bridleway' and 'Grambler Farm'. Go through a wooden gate by the farm and continue to an open area. Bear left here and follow a path between hedges. Shortly join a track and head onwards to a clearing. Bear left here to take the path on the left. At a junction with a track turn left.

3. Look to your right for a field gateway with breeze block gateposts and go through it. Cross a stile at the next gate and then keep straight ahead across the next field. Cross two more stiles and continue between wire fences by a

house to a final stile. Walk down a lane to a junction of surfaced roads and then follow the road opposite for 100yds (91m) to Gwennap Pit.

4. Follow the road away from Gwennap Pit. Ignore the first few turn-offs, and in about 300yds (274m), just after some barns on the left, turn right along a broad track, signposted 'Public Bridleway'. Where the track swings sharply to the right, head straight up a path between hedges. Head on over a crossing then, at a second crossing beside a ruined building, turn right along a stony track to the prominent summit of Carn Marth.

5. Pass a flooded quarry on your left, then follow a rocky path round to the right of a trig point and on along the fenced-in rim of a deep quarry. Keep left at a fork and go down a track to reach a surfaced road. Turn left and in 30yds (27m) turn left again along a track beside two large tanks. Follow the track along to a T-junction with the main road at a house called Tara. Cross the road with great care, turn right and continue for 300yds (180m).

6. Ignore the first public bridleway, after about 150yds (137m), and then go left down a path between houses, signposted 'Public Bridleway'. Continue along past a lane on the right to reach a junction with Trefusis Road. Turn right and then left into Raymond Road. Turn right at the next crossroads into Sea View Terrace. Turn left down Wesley Street and then on into Fore Street.

Where to eat and drink
You can picnic in Gwennap Pit, but please don't leave any litter. Redruth has several pleasant restaurants, cafés and pubs to choose from. Sample the wonderful local Cornish pasties from Rowe's Cornish Bakers in Fore Street. The Red Lion pub is also in Fore Street, as is a fish and chip shop.

What to see
The field hedgerows throughout the walk are bright with wild flowers in spring and summer. Butterflies brighten the scene even more. Look for the handsome peacock butterfly (*Nymphalidae*) that feeds on the nectar of bramble flowers and also on the juice of berries. The brownish-red peacock is easily identified by the 'peacock-eye' markings on its hind wings.

While you're there
A visit to Gwennap Pit and its visitor centre is irresistible, but Redruth itself deserves exploration. Many buildings in Fore Street are Victorian Gothic and have unusual features, such as decorative brickwork. These, and the Italianate clock tower of 1828, reflect the boom period of Redruth's growth. The Pednandrea Mine Chimney Stack was part of a mine that operated from about 1710 to 1891 producing copper, tin, lead and arsenic. The original height of the stack was between 126 and 140ft (38 and 43m).

FROM CHAPEL PORTH TO TOWAN CROSS

DISTANCE/TIME	2.5 miles (4km) / 1hr 30min
ASCENT/GRADIENT	295ft (90m) / ▲ ▲
PATHS	Stony underfoot on cliff top, otherwise good; may be muddy in valley bottom
LANDSCAPE	Dramatic, desolate mining landscape and lush green valley
SUGGESTED MAP	OS Explorer 104 Redruth & St Agnes
START/FINISH	Grid reference: SW697494
DOG FRIENDLINESS	Off lead but under control. No dogs on Chapel Porth beach
PARKING	Chapel Porth car park (National Trust)
PUBLIC TOILETS	Chapel Porth car park
NOTES	On one short coastal section, the path is close to the edge of unfenced cliff – take particular care with young children and dogs

The area surrounding the seaside village of St Agnes and its neighbouring cove of Chapel Porth has a dramatic history of tin and copper mining. Even the car park at Chapel Porth, from where this walk begins, was once crammed full of mine buildings and industrial activity. In the 19th century, Chapel Coombe, the tranquil and deeply vegetated stream valley behind the cove, was wreathed in smoke and rang with the sounds of mine processing.

In spite of all this industrial activity it is only from the cliff top that you can see the scarred ground, spoil heaps and ruined walls of Victorian mining. Much of the area is now in the care of the National Trust, and perhaps the most surprising aspect of this landscape is that it is of national importance for its wild flowers and plants, because of its designation as a classic coastal heath and maritime habitat. Windblown sand carried up from the long swathes of beach below the cliffs enriches the soil with natural lime, providing the perfect environment for myriad plants such as low-lying heath bedstraw and thyme. Heath bedstraw is identified by its small spear-shaped leaves and tiny white flowers. Thyme has small dark green leaves and tight clusters of purple-pink flowers.

On the heathland behind the cliffs, bell heather, cross-leafed heath and western gorse make a beautiful mosaic of colour, especially in autumn. In this kind of habitat you should also spot the tiny yellow-headed tormentil and the blue-flowered milkwort. The lovely heath spotted orchid also grows amidst the heather and gorse, as does eyebright, with its small but distinctive purple-veined white flowers. Enjoy the contrast of the peace and quiet amid the sheltering trees of the Chapel Coombe valley. Here you should look out for small songbirds like wren, stonechat, chaffinch and willow warbler among the hawthorn, blackthorn, willow and sycamore trees.

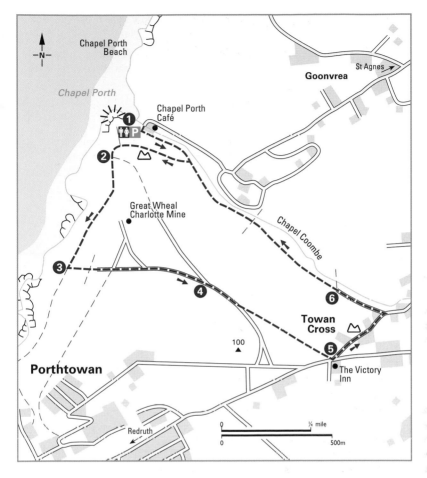

1. From the back of the car park cross a wooden bridge over a stream and follow a path inland beside the stream. After about 0.25 miles (400m), at a junction, turn sharply right and follow a stony track uphill. At a junction of tracks (acorn signpost) on the cliff top, keep ahead along a broad, stony track, parallel to the coast.

2. Follow the track through heaps of waste stone below the ruins of Great Wheal Charlotte mine stack. Keep ahead along the coast path. Take care with young children and dogs on a short section near the unfenced cliff edge.

3. The coast path reaches a junction with a path coming in from Wheal Charlotte at a sharp angle from the left. Don't join this, but follow a narrow path that runs directly inland then, at a junction, go ahead along a wide track.

4. Bear right along a wide stony track at the next junction. Reach another junction and bear off left along a subsidiary track. Reach the main road opposite the Victory Inn.

5. Turn left across a lay-by and a grassy verge, opposite the Victory Inn, and bear left down a surfaced lane. Descend quite steeply (watch for any traffic on

narrow sections). Near the valley bottom and just before some houses, turn off left along a shaded, unsurfaced lane, signed 'Public Bridleway'.

6. At a junction with a path, bear off left and keep to the path along Chapel Coombe. Follow this through trees at first, and keep straight ahead to return to the car park at Chapel Porth.

Where to eat and drink

The Victory Inn at Towan Cross has a varied menu and also offers snacks. It's known for its good selection of real ales. In the car park above the beach, the Chapel Porth Café is open daily from April to October, and is usually open on Fridays and at weekends, and in school holidays from November until March. It serves hot and cold drinks, breakfasts, lunch, snacks and ice creams.

What to see

During the summer look out for butterflies along the sea cliffs and on the heathland. You may spot the painted lady, a beautiful butterfly with orange and black markings and with white spots on the tip of its fore-wings. The grayling is a brown butterfly with black edgings on its wings and white, eye-like spots on its fore-wings.

While you're there

Go for a stroll on the sand at Chapel Porth – but be warned, this is a tidal beach and the incoming tide can cover it very rapidly. Check for details on notices and with lifeguards. You should never enter any caves at the base of the cliffs.

ON ST AGNES BEACON

DISTANCE/TIME	5 miles (8km) / 2hrs
ASCENT/GRADIENT	623ft (190m) / ▲ ▲
PATHS	Good coastal footpaths and inland tracks
LANDSCAPE	Dramatic coastal cliffs and a high heath-covered hill
SUGGESTED MAP	OS Explorer 104 Redruth & St Agnes
START/FINISH	Grid reference: SW699514
DOG FRIENDLINESS	Dogs on lead through grazed areas. No dogs on Chapel Porth beach
PARKING	St Agnes Head. Several car parks close to clifftop track. Start the walk from any of these
PUBLIC TOILETS	Chapel Porth Beach

The breathtaking sea cliffs of St Agnes Head are well hidden from above. There is no easy view of them, unless you are a very skilled rock climber. On St Agnes Head and on Carn Gowla, the cliff that runs south from the headland, vast 300ft (90m) high walls of rock soar from a restless sea. They do not end at clear-cut edges, however. Instead they merge with steep slopes of grass and heather that in turn rise steeply to the cliff top.

This walk takes you along clifftop tracks past the little promontory of Tubby's Head, once an Iron-Age settlement fortified by an earth embankment across its neck. From here you pass through what was once an industrial landscape, where the ruins of mine buildings evoke Cornwall's great era of mineral mining. One such building is the impressive Towanroath engine house, a lofty granite edifice that has been restored by the National Trust. Built in 1872, this was the pumping house for the Wheal Coates mine, whose buildings you can see when walking along the coast path. Flooding of the deeper Cornish mines was always a problem, and pumping houses were built to draw up water and eject it through tunnels known as adits in the cliff face below.

Beyond Towanroath the path descends into Chapel Porth, where you can enjoy the delights of a typical Cornish beach, although it is diminished at high tide and attention should be paid to safety warnings. During the 19th century the entire valley floor that leads down to the cove was given over to the processing of the mineral ore that came from the numerous tin and copper mines, scattered across the surrounding landscape. As you walk up the valley, you pick your way through a landscape now overgrown, but that was once subdued by industry. From the valley floor the route follows a smaller valley that is protected from the harsh onshore weather by high ground. Soon you climb on to the bare, rounded summit of St Agnes Beacon, 629ft (192m) high and a superb viewpoint. As the name makes clear, this prominent hilltop was used traditionally for the lighting of signal fires and for celebratory bonfires. From the Beacon's airy heights you drop down to the coast once more.

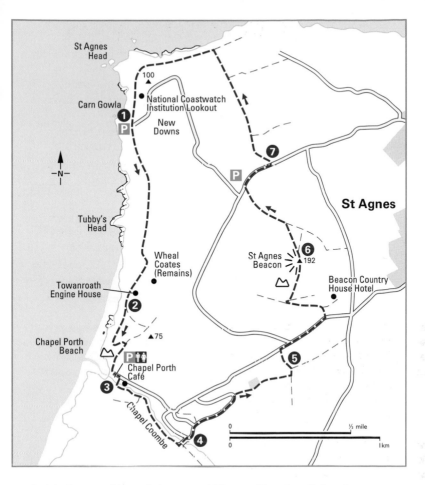

1. Join the coastal footpath from your clifftop parking place. Follow the stony track across Tubby's Head. Branch off right on to a narrower path (acorn signpost) about 100yds (91m) before old mine buildings (Wheal Coates mine). Cross a stone stile and continue to Towanroath mine engine house.

2. About 80yds (71m) beyond Towanroath, branch off right at a junction and continue to Chapel Porth Beach.

3. Cross the stream at the back corner of the car park and follow a path up Chapel Coombe. Keep straight ahead when the main path bends sharply right. Pass below a mine building and, where the path forks among trees, go left and over a short footbridge.

4. Turn right along a track and, where it bends left beyond Chapel Porth Farm gate, go right along another track. In 50yds (45m) keep ahead at a junction. After passing some houses the track becomes a path. Keep ahead at a fork. Go through a gateway, follow the field-edge, then turn left through a kissing gate onto a wide track.

5. At a junction, turn left and then right at Willow Cottage and go up to a public road. Turn right and keep ahead at the next junction. In 300yds (274m),

next to the entrance of the Beacon Country House Hotel, go up a stony track on the left, signed 'The Beacon'. After 75yds (69m), at a junction, turn left. The track becomes a path just past a cottage. At a staggered junction keep straight uphill to the summit of St Agnes Beacon.

6. From the summit of the Beacon take the left of two tracks then shortly afterwards follow the left-hand track of two again, heading northwest down to a road. Turn right along the road to reach a seat.

7. Go down the track opposite the seat. Where the track bends right, keep straight on down a path directly to the edge of the cliffs, then turn left at a junction with the coast path and return to the car park.

Where to eat and drink

There is a café at Chapel Porth, at the midway point of the walk. It's open daily in the summer and from Friday to Sunday between November and March. St Agnes village has a couple of good pubs where you can get bar meals.

What to see

In summer the heathery vegetation of the St Agnes cliff tops and the inland hill of the Beacon attract a wealth of butterflies such as the grayling, a brown-coloured butterfly distinguished by the black edges to its wings and the two white-pupilled spots on its fore-wings. It feeds on wild thyme and heather and often perches on the rocks. Another butterfly to look out for here is the green hairstreak. It is golden brown on its upper wings and distinctively green on its underside.

While you're there

St Agnes has many features, including a picturesque terrace of houses known as Stippy Stappy, the St Agnes Museum and a beach at Trevaunance Cove. The Coastwatch Lookout at St Agnes Head can be visited when a notice is displayed.

FROM PORTREATH
TO TEHIDY WOODS

DISTANCE/TIME	4 miles (6.4km) / 3hrs
ASCENT/GRADIENT	459ft (140m) / ▲
PATHS	Good coastal path, woodland path, farm tracks
LANDSCAPE	Precipitous sea cliffs and deep woodland
SUGGESTED MAP	OS Explorer 104 Redruth & St Agnes
START/FINISH	Grid reference: SW654453
DOG FRIENDLINESS	Dogs on lead through grazed areas
PARKING	Portreath Beach; Basset's Cove; North Cliffs; Tehidy Country Park; East Lodge
PUBLIC TOILETS	Portreath and East Lodge Car Park

The sea cliffs near Portreath in mid-Cornwall are made up of unstable shale and sandstone. Yet their very friability lends them to the formation of fantastic offshore islands and ridges of marginally harder rock. From the edge of the cliffs a flat platform of land, Carvannel Downs, once submerged beneath the sea, runs inland. It is a featureless landscape except where the dark curtain of Tehidy Woods breaks the profile.

There can be no greater contrast than that between the bare, windswept cliffs and the enfolding trees, and this walk samples both environments. The walk starts from Portreath's popular beach and harbour (see While you're there), and soon leads onto the awesome cliffs to the west of the village. You stroll along the edge of the flat, heath-covered Carvannel Downs, aware always of the 260ft (80m) cliffs only a few steps away. Below lie vast rock islands dotting the inaccessible sands of Western Cove.

The Horse is a breathtaking ridge of rock and grass that projects from the cliff face and makes up the east wall of Ralph's Cupboard, a vast, dizzying gulf that belies the quaintness of its name and that is said to be the remains of a huge cavern whose roof collapsed. Do not be tempted to go too near the edge of the cliffs, especially in windy weather. Far ahead you can see Godrevy Lighthouse on its rocky island.

Beyond Ralph's Cupboard, a name that may derive from a one-time smuggler, or from an old Cornish word, the path leads steeply down into Porthcadjack Cove. Here a thin stream of water pours over the lower cliff edge, where 19th-century smugglers used to hoist their contraband from the beach using elaborate pulley-systems.

Beyond, above Basset's Cove, the route turns inland and draws you into the enfolding trees of Tehidy Woods, once the estate of the Basset family, who were famous mine owners. The Bassets planted extensive woodlands around their Georgian house, and these now mature woods still offer shelter and security after the exhilarating exposure of the cliffs.

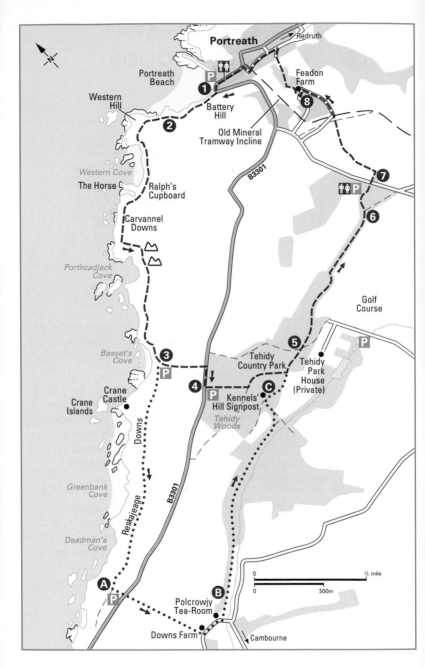

1. Turn right to cross the bridge opposite the car park and then right up Battery Hill, signposted 'Coast Path'. Follow the lane uphill to its end at houses above the beach. Go left in front of garages, signposted 'Coast Path Gwithian'.

2. Follow the path through a gate and then keep straight uphill to the cliff top. Don't go too close to the cliff edge. Turn left and follow the path round the cliff

edge above Ralph's Cupboard. Continue by steep paths into and out of Porthcadjack Cove.

3. Reach a car parking area above Basset's Cove. Follow the broad track inland, then at the public road, cross over and turn right for a short distance.

4. Turn left through the North Cliffs car park and continue down a tree-lined track. Turn left at a T-junction and keep on the main track, ignoring branches to the left and right, to reach another T-junction by houses. Turn left along a broad track.

5. Keep ahead on the main track to reach a junction and four-way signpost. (A café can be reached in 0.25 miles (400m) down the right-hand signposted track.) On the main route, keep straight on, signposted 'East Lodge'. Reach a junction by a seat. Go right and continue along the track beside the golf course.

6. About 40yds (37m) beyond the end of the golf course section, at a junction, bear off left into woods, signposted 'East Lodge Car Park' and 'Portreath'. Stay on the main path to soon reach the car park and a public road.

7. Cross the road diagonally right and then go left, following the sign 'Mining Trail', between wooden posts with red marks. At a four-way signpost, just before chalets, keep ahead and follow a surfaced road to the bottom of the hill.

8. Turn left, then in a few paces turn right down a concrete track. At a farmyard go sharp left by a public footpath sign and follow a path down through woods, keeping to the main path, to reach a surfaced road. Just past 'Glenfeadon Castle' turn left, pass beneath a bridge, then at a junction keep ahead along Tregea Terrace and back to Portreath Beach car park.

Extending the walk This extension to the main walk continues along the cliff tops past Basset's Cove at waypoint 3. Keep straight across the bottom edge of the car parking area and keep on following the coast path, past the remains of Crane Castle. Just beyond Greenbank Cove and Deadman's Cove you reach a small car parking area, Point A, close to the road. Go inland to the road here and cross it with care, then go over a stile and follow the edge of a field downhill and between thorn trees. This path leads to a road where you turn left for about 120yds (110m). Turn left at the Polcrowjy Tea-Room, and follow a track into the Tehidy Country Park at Point B. Follow the broad drive through the trees, then take the left-hand branch uphill. At a T-junction turn left uphill and reach another T-junction at a signpost, Point C. Turn right here, signposted 'East Lodge' and follow the broad track to reach waypoint 5 on the main walk.

Where to eat and drink

There is a café at the south entrance to Tehidy Woods. Follow the sign from waypoint 5. In Portreath there are several cafés. The Basset Arms pub on the south side of the river is passed at the end of the walk.

While you're there

Portreath harbour and docks still give some idea of their industrial past. The original fishing cove was turned into a harbour in the 1760s. Copper ore was exported from here. By the 1830s a railway connected Portreath with Hayle and the mines.

LELANT TO ST IVES

DISTANCE/TIME	4 miles (6.4km) / 2hrs 30min
ASCENT/GRADIENT	180ft (55m) / ▲
PATHS	Excellent
LANDSCAPE	Coastal sand dunes, cliff paths and surfaced lanes
SUGGESTED MAP	AA Walker's Map 10 Land's End & The Lizard
START	Grid reference: SW546373
FINISH	Grid reference: SW519401
DOG FRIENDLINESS	Can let dogs off lead. Summer dog bans on Carbis Bay Beach and Porthminster Beach
PARKING	Station car park, St Ives, or other car parks throughout town. There is very limited parking outside Lelant. The advised option is to catch a train from St Ives to Lelant and walk back to St Ives.
PUBLIC TOILETS	Carbis Bay and Porthminster Beach

In 1877 the archetypal Cornish fishing village of St Ives was linked to the mainline railway and was never the same again. The 4.5 miles (7.2km) of track that wound its way from St Erth along the estuary of the River Hayle and then above St Ives Bay was intended to make markets more accessible to the local fishing industry. It also opened the town to the fast-developing tourism of the late 19th century. Fishing declined, but by the 1940s and 1950s the branch line was carrying tens of thousands of holidaymakers to St Ives and was enjoyed by huge numbers of local people. Today the line carries crowds of day-visitors and its scenic qualities are still unspoiled. The coastal footpath also traverses the beautiful surroundings through which the line passes. You can travel either way between station halts and return on foot through magnificent scenery.

St Ives probably originated as a small fishing community as far back as prehistory. It prospered greatly from the medieval period and the pilchard fishing that became its mainstay helped to create the distinctive area known as Downlong, whose cobbled streets weave around the town's harbour. St Ives is now one of Europe's most famous resorts, and has the distinction of being an internationally acclaimed centre of art. The town's numerous art galleries, headed by the prestigious Tate Gallery St Ives, enhance that reputation.

This walk approaches St Ives along the line of the railway on the southern shore of St Ives Bay. It begins at the charming station of Lelant, a peaceful little place on the inner estuary of the Hayle River. From Lelant station the route leads to the handsome church of St Uny and St Anta at Lelant, briefly crosses a golf course and then skirts above Porth Kidney, where a vast expanse of sand is exposed at low water. At Hawke's Point, the path enters a green and leafy section of coast and soon reaches the popular resort of

Carbis Bay. The railway is crossed by a footbridge just beyond here and before reaching the outskirts of St Ives the way leads past a fascinating relic of the pilchard fishing industry, the Baulking House. From here a lookout, called a 'huer', kept watch for the tell-tale purple stain of pilchard shoals in the bay below. The huer would then use hand-held signalling devices to direct the seine-net boats in the silent, skilful trapping of many thousands of the fish that was the good fortune of St Ives for centuries.

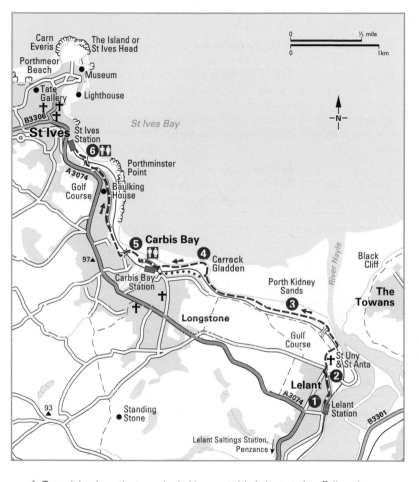

1. Turn right along the tree-shaded lane outside Lelant station. Follow the surfaced lane, keeping straight ahead at a junction, and in just under 0.25 miles (400m) reach a T-junction. Turn right and uphill to the Church of St Uny and St Anta.

2. Take the obvious footpath to the left of the churchyard entrance. The path leads for a short distance across part of a golf course. (Look out for flying golf balls.) Continue until a concrete blockhouse is reached. Go under the railway bridge, then turn left by a house, at a coast path sign. There was once a small ferry running from shore to shore here.

3. The way now leads above the sand dunes of Porth Kidney, where a glittering expanse of sand is exposed at low tide. Soon you climb steadily between hedges to the headland of Carrack Gladden, or Hawke's Point. Just past a railway crossing you have a choice of routes.

4. Keeping to the higher route leads alongside the railway to Carbis Bay. For a more scenic route take the signposted right-hand branch steeply downhill and along the grassy cliff edge, finally climbing some steep steps to meet the road. Turn right here and down to Carbis Bay beach and the promise of a swim in warm weather.

5. Follow the path in front of the Carbis Bay Hotel, then turn up left to climb steps to reach a footbridge across the railway. Follow the path ahead and on along a surfaced lane that runs through a residential area. Where the lane branches, keep straight ahead, signposted 'Coast Path', to reach the Baulking House. Go straight across at a crossroads just past the Baulking House and follow a track past several seats and then cross a bridge over a railway. Continue along this path, ignoring steps to the left. The path becomes a track and then a lane.

6. Where the lane bends sharply left, keep ahead – signed 'St Ives' – and go down a surfaced path, and then some steps, to reach Porthminster Beach by the Porthminster Beach Café. Walk alongside the beach and reach St Ives railway station and car park by going up steps in the high granite wall on the left. Alternatively, keep ahead past the Pedn Olva Hotel and walk into the heart of the town.

Where to eat and drink

At Carbis Bay there is a café on the beach and a shop selling ice cream. The Carbis Bay Hotel just above the beach does bar meals. The award-winning Porthminster Beach Café is a charming art deco building with a balcony overlooking Porthminster Beach. St Ives town has several traditional inns and a great number of cafés and restaurants.

What to see

Cormorants haunt the mouth of the Hayle River and can often be seen, perching on the wooden poles that mark the seaward channel of the estuary, their wings outspread. They are not drying their wings, but do this as an aid to digestion. Cormorants and shags are often mistaken for each other. The cormorant is much bigger and has a distinguishing white patch under its chin. You are more likely to spot cormorants in and around estuaries and they often fly far inland to freshwater lakes.

While you're there

Lelant's Church of St Uny and St Anta has an intriguing history. Records suggest that a 5th- or 6th-century chapel once stood between the present church and the sea, but that it was buried by the encroaching sands. The present church has Norman features and was once the focus of the medieval village of Lelant, the main port of the area, until silt and sand made the estuary difficult to navigate.

ST IVES AND CLODGY POINT

DISTANCE/TIME	8 miles (12.9km) / 4hrs
ASCENT/GRADIENT	394ft (120m) / ▲
PATHS	Coastal path, can be quite rocky. Field paths, many stiles
LANDSCAPE	Very scenic coast and small inland fields
SUGGESTED MAP	AA Walker's Map 10 Land's End & The Lizard
START/FINISH	Grid reference: SW522408
DOG FRIENDLINESS	Dogs on lead through grazed areas; no dogs on beaches Easter Sunday to 1 October
PARKING	The Island car park, St Ives
PUBLIC TOILETS	Dove Street near start of walk, Smeaton's Pier, Porthgwidden Beach and Porthmeor Beach
NOTES	There are no refreshment points on the route once you leave St Ives, but the town has numerous pubs, restaurants and takeaways

In the days before modern transport, the scenic road from St Ives to St Just, along the north coast of the Land's End peninsula, was no more than a rough track used for carrying heavier loads by cart and wagon, horse or donkey. Even before this track evolved people travelled more easily on foot along the coastal belt below the hills, through land that still retains evidence of ancient Bronze Age fields. Until the early 20th century the field paths, with their sturdy punctuation marks of granite stiles, were used by local people to visit each other and to travel to church and to the market at St Ives.

The coastal paths on the outer edge of the ancient fields barely existed in earlier times. But as commerce and foreign wars increased, the coastline of southwest England especially came under much closer scrutiny by the authorities. When 19th-century smuggling was at its height, government 'revenue men' patrolled as best they could the wilder reaches of the coast to foil the 'freetraders'. In later years the coastguard service also patrolled the coast on foot until there were few sections that were not passable, by footpath at least. Linking these paths to create a continuous route for the walker was the final stage in the evolution of today's coastal footpath.

This walk starts from the middle of St Ives and heads west along the glorious coastline, once watched so assiduously. This is a very remote and wild part of the west Cornwall coast, a landscape of exquisite colours in spring and summer and where the steep and vegetated cliffs are not breached until the narrow Treveal Valley breaks through to the sea at River Cove. Here the route turns inland and plunges instantly into a lush, green countryside that seems, at times, far removed from the sea. Field paths lead unswervingly back towards St Ives, with a sequence of granite stiles reminding you of a very different world when this journey was an everyday event for Cornish folk.

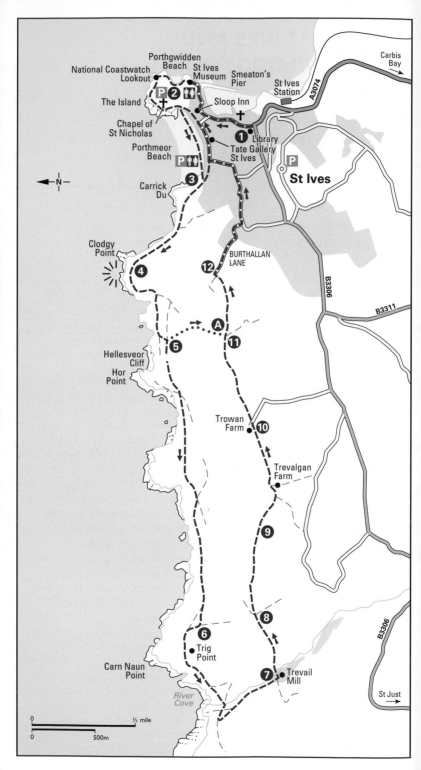

Carbis
Bay

National Coastwatch
Lookout

Porthgwidden
Beach

St Ives
Museum

Smeaton's
Pier

St Ives
Station

A3074

The Island

Sloop Inn

Chapel of
St Nicholas

②

①

Library

Porthmeor
Beach

Tate Gallery
St Ives

St Ives

P

③

Carrick
Du

Clodgy
Point

④

BURTHALLAN
LANE

⑫

B3306

B3311

Ⓐ

⑤

⑪

Hellesveor
Cliff

Hor
Point

Trowan
Farm

⑩

Trevalgan
Farm

⑨

⑧

⑥

Trig
Point

⑦

Trevail
Mill

Carn Naun
Point

River
Cove

St Just
→

B3306

0   ½ mile

0   500m

1. Starting at the library, walk north, past a Co-op supermarket, and bear right. Pass left in front of the parish church and continue ahead on a narrow shopping street full of small independent shops and eateries. Follow this along to the beach. Walk along the harbourfront towards Smeaton's Pier. Just before the pier entrance, turn left, signed to 'St Ives Museum'. Where the road bends, keep straight on into Wheal Dream. Turn right past St Ives Museum, then follow a walkway to Porthgwidden Beach.

2. Cross the car park above the beach and climb to the National Coastwatch lookout. Go down steps behind the building at the back of the lookout, then follow a footway to Porthmeor Beach. Go along the beach. At the beach end, go up to the car park. (The Tate St Ives Gallery is just down the road to the left.)

3. Go up steps beside the New Saints Boardriders Clubhouse, then turn right along a surfaced track past putting and bowling greens. Continue to the rocky headlands of Carrick Du and then Clodgy Point.

4. From Clodgy Point walk uphill and follow the path round to the right. Continue along a boggy and very rocky path. In about 0.5 miles (800m) take the left path uphill at a junction by a large lichen-covered boulder.

5. At a T-junction with a track just past a National Trust sign for 'Hellesveor Cliff', turn right and follow the coast path for 1.5 miles (2.4km). Just after a gate and stream, keep straight ahead.

6. Keep right along the coast path at a junction just past a shed and a ruin to your left. Cross Carn Naun Point. Continue past a trig point and descend to River Cove. Cross a granite footbridge to a gate and turn right at a T-junction. Climb to where the path levels off at a junction and follow the inland path, signposted 'River Cove & Field Path'.

7. At a junction with a track, go left through a kissing gate, then follow signs past Trevail Mill. Go through another kissing gate and climb steadily.

8. Cross a track and follow the hedged-in path, signposted 'Bridleway'. In about 40yds (36m) go left over a stile into a field. Follow field-edges ahead over intervening stiles

9. Keep alongside the right-hand hedge in the field with a granite upright. Cross a stile. Keep to the field edge between the hedge and an electrified fence. Go over a stile beside the second of two field gates. Follow the hedge along and continue to Trevalgan Farm. Cross a large stone stile to go between buildings and in 50yds (46m), turn left at a gate and then follow the copious handmade signs to cross a stile. Continue along to Trowan Farm.

10. At Trowan Farm, pass a granite post by a handmade 'Footpath' sign; continue between houses, then go through a field gateway straight ahead. Follow field paths over several stiles to Point A.

11. Cross a lane, then a stile, and follow a path between hedges then the left-edges of small fields. Pass a field gap on the left and turn left, as signed, just before another gap. Go through a gate and cross two stiles to pass between high hedges to a surfaced lane.

12. Turn right (Burthallan Lane) to a T-junction with the main road. Turn left and follow the road downhill to Porthmeor Beach.

Shortening the walk This shorter version of the walk follows the main route from St Ives Harbour. As you climb over the Island, waypoint 2, divert to the little Chapel of St Nicholas, on the summit. Follow the main walk past the rocky headlands of Carrick Du and Clodgy Point and continue round the edge of the cliffs to waypoint 5, where this shortened version of the walk turns inland at a small granite marker post signed 'Hellesveor 3/4 mile'. The headland just ahead of this junction is Hor Point. In the 1950s, long before public consciousness was quite so attuned to environmentalism, St Ives Council put forward plans to use Hor Point for tipping rubbish. This reflected the traditional attitude of earlier generations that wilderness sea cliffs were out of sight and out of mind and were thus exploitable for everything from quarrying to rubbish disposal. (Also around this time a proposal to site a nuclear power station on the beautiful Zennor Moors, above the coast, was rejected.) Hor Point was saved from ruin because the landowner, faced with potential compulsory purchase of the point by the council, sold it instead to the National Trust and the rubbish tip plan was soon shelved. With the preserved beauty of the coast and moors in mind, you turn left and inland at waypoint 5, to follow a hedged-in track that is probably centuries old. Such tracks gave access to the cliff, where animals were grazed and where stone was gathered for building and furze for fuel. When the path joins a wide track, continue for 150yds (140m) to reach a bend where a footpath crosses with a sign denoting that a right turn here leads back to 'Trowan'. This is Point A, Point 11 on the main walk. Turn left across the stile, on to the main route, and follow the last part of the old field path back to St Ives as detailed on the main walk.

Where to eat and drink
There are no refreshment points on the route once you leave St Ives, but the town has numerous pubs, restaurants and takeaways. The Sloop Inn, midway along the harbourfront, is a famous harbourside inn that does pub food and is usually very busy. Just past the Sloop is the Cornish Pasty Shop, where you can buy delicious pasties.

What to see
Both versions of this walk pass close to the Chapel of St Nicholas – an unmissable feature gracing the headland known as the Island. The chapel dates from the 16th century, when it was used not only as a seaman's chapel but also as an early form of lighthouse. In later years it was used as a lookout by revenue men on the watch for smugglers.

While you're there
St Ives Museum portrays the history and culture of St Ives with considerable panache. The splendid Tate Gallery St Ives is a custom-built gallery and celebrates the work of the mainly Modernist St Ives painters. There is a café inside. No dogs, except guide dogs, are allowed.

THE ZENNOR COAST

DISTANCE/TIME	3.5 miles (5.6km) / 2hr 30min
ASCENT/GRADIENT	260ft (80m) / ▲ ▲ ▲
PATHS	Occasionally rocky on coast path; some steep steps to descend (handrails); paths may be muddy; many stiles
LANDSCAPE	Rugged coast and small fields below rocky moorland
SUGGESTED MAP	AA Walker's Map 10 Land's End & The Lizard
START/FINISH	Grid reference: SW453385
DOG FRIENDLINESS	Lead required through fields
PARKING	Zennor car park
PUBLIC TOILETS	None on route

The Zennor area of West Cornwall is famous for a legend of a mermaid so enamoured with the singing of a local youth that she enticed him into the waters of nearby Pendour Cove. This walk takes you along the cliffs above the cove, where you should keep your eyes open for seals rather than mermaids. The real Zennor transcends this charming fantasy, not least because of the beauty of its location on a narrow coastal shelf between the Atlantic cliffs and the hills of the Land's End Peninsula. Within the village itself are such features as the Church of St Senara, parts of which date from the Norman period and the 15th century. The church has a splendid three-stage tower that dominates the scene. The mermaid legend is given even greater prominence by a fine carved bench-end of the said charmer in all her glory.

The narrow coastal shelf here is barely a mile (1.6km) wide. It represents a classic example of a wave-cut platform that once lay beneath the sea and was later left high and dry as sea levels fell. The hills above Zennor are studded with huge granite slabs and rocks, and in the small, flat fields around the village you can see the rounded tops of massive boulders protruding from the grass. The boundaries of these fields were first formed during the Iron Age, and the granite walls, or 'hedges' as they are called in west Cornwall, that still separate the fields today create a random web-like pattern that makes the area very distinctive. These Cornish hedges are made up of two walls of granite stones, with the space between filled with earth that supports an outer pelt of grass and vivid wild flowers. Somewhere beneath the coastal fields lies the boundary between the moorland granite and the more ancient rocks of the nearby coast, the greenstone and slate that make up the dramatic coal-black cliffs that rise for over 200ft (61m) from the restless sea.

The narrow lane that takes you down from Zennor village meets the coastal footpath. The first part of the walk circles Zennor Head, the most dramatic feature of this section of coast. There was mineral mining here during the 19th century, and mill wheels once ground corn beside the tumbling stream that falls into Pendour Cove, although few traces of these past industries survive today. From the high ground west of Pendour you can see the great cliffs of Zennor Head across the bay, their walls jet black in colour and mottled with patches of green lichen. The path wriggles its way along the cliff top to the lesser headland of Carnelloe, from where the walk leads inland and then back to Zennor along an ancient field path. This path is part of the 'highway' between farmsteads and hamlets once used by local people, on foot and at a genuinely human pace.

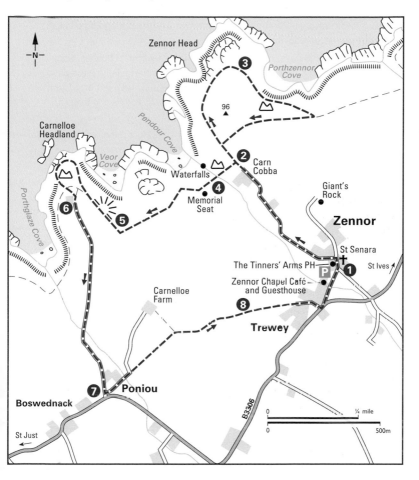

1. Turn left out of the car park, pass The Tinners' Arms, then turn left again and bear round left down a lane behind the pub. Follow the lane for just over 0.5 miles (800m) to where it ends by an entrance to a house. Keep straight ahead along a narrow path for about 60yds (55m). Cross a stile onto a junction with the coast path beside a National Trust sign for Zennor Head.

2. Keep straight ahead along the coast path towards Zennor Head. Reach the summit of the Head, where there is a National Trust memorial plaque set into a large rock. Continue round to the right along the coast path, pass a cluster of large rocks, and then descend steeply.

3. Follow the path (it is close to the cliff edge in places, so take care) and climb steeply to a junction beside a small granite footpath sign. Turn right and follow a narrow path high above the sea and across the neck of Zennor Head. Turn left at a T-junction and retrace your earlier steps to where you joined the coast path at waypoint 2, by the National Trust sign for Zennor Head. Turn right and descend quite steeply and, just by a bench, descend steep steps (handrail). Descend a final flight of steps to a wooden bridge across a stream that gushes over boulders to Pendour Cove below.

4. Keeping left immediately at a fork, follow the rocky path steeply uphill, and pass a memorial seat. Continue uphill, ignoring a minor path going off right. The path levels off above Veor Cove.

5. Cross a stile and pass through a long stand of blackthorn bushes. Soon start to descend the northeast side of Carnelloe Headland. Follow the path round the base of the headland and turn steeply uphill. Turn left at a T-junction and signpost below a house, and climb steadily uphill. Follow the footpath behind the house to reach an open grassy area.

6. Join a wide grassy track and follow it inland, passing a mine wheel pit down the slope on the right. Reach a junction by a stream. Go through a kissing gate and keep left along a track.

7. Just before the main road, at Poniou, go left along a track in front of houses. Cross a bridge over a stream, and in 30yds (27m), where the track veers sharp left, bear off it and cross a grid stile to the left of a gate. Follow the left edge of a field and continue through several fields and over stiles.

8. Cross the final field and go over a stile and along a path between a hedge and a wire fence. Cross a final stile and follow a grassy track towards farm buildings. Turn right along a concrete track through Trewey Farm. At the main road turn left, with care, and in a few paces, at a junction, keep left and steeply downhill to return to the car park.

Where to eat and drink

The Tinners' Arms at Zennor is a famous institution once beloved of D H Lawrence. It has a restaurant and lovely garden area and does pub food. Just by the car park is the cheerful Zennor Chapel Café and Guesthouse, offering hot drinks, soup, baguettes, paninis and salads.

What to see

On the field section of the walk you'll cross a number of flat stiles made up of long granite steps laid at the same level and with gaps between. These are called 'Coffen' stiles, from the old Cornish word for a hole or depression in the ground.

While you're there

Visit Zennor's handsome church of St Senara, from which the village derives its name. Though most of the church dates back to the 13th and 15th centuries, there are also some Norman features and it stands on the site of a church built in the sixth century, reputedly by St Senara herself. Look for the carved mermaid bench-end.

EXPLORING PENDEEN AND ITS MINES

DISTANCE/TIME	5 miles (8km) / 4hrs
ASCENT/GRADIENT	328ft (100m) / ▲
PATHS	Coastal footpath, field paths and moorland tracks
LANDSCAPE	Spectacular coastal cliffs, old mining country and open moorland
SUGGESTED MAP	AA Walker's Map 10 Land's End & The Lizard
START/FINISH	Grid reference: SW383344
DOG FRIENDLINESS	Keep dogs on lead in field sections
PARKING	Free car park in centre of Pendeen village, opposite Boscaswell Stores, on the B3306
PUBLIC TOILETS	Pendeen car park and Geevor Tin Mine

The tin and copper mines of Pendeen on the north coast of the Land's End Peninsula are redundant; the culmination of the long decline of Cornish coastal mining since its Victorian heyday. The deep mining of Cornwall lost out to cheap ore from surface strip mines in Asia and to the vagaries of the international market. At Pendeen the area's last working mine of Geevor closed in 1990 after years of uncertainty and false promise, and despite vigorous efforts by the local community to save it. Today, the modern buildings of Geevor have been transformed into a fascinating mining museum, but it is the ruined granite chimney stacks and engine houses of the 19th-century industry that have given this mining coast its dramatic visual heritage.

Early in the walk you reach the Geevor Tin Mine and then the National Trust's Levant Mine and Beam Engine (see While you're there). From Levant the coast path runs on to Botallack, where the famous Crown's Mine Engine Houses stand on a spectacular shelf of rock above the Atlantic. The tunnels and galleries of the Crown's Mine ran out for almost 1 mile (1.6km) beneath the sea, and the mine was entered down an angled runway using wagons. You can visit the Crown's Mine Engine Houses by following a series of tracks down towards the sea from the main walk. Flooding was a constant problem for these mines, and some of the earliest steam engines were developed to pump water from the workings. On the cliff top above the Crown's Mine the National Trust has restored the 19th-century façade of the Botallack Count House. This was the assaying and administrative centre for all the surrounding mines.

From the Count House the way leads to the old mining villages of Botallack and Carnyorth, before climbing steadily inland to the moorland hills of Carnyorth Common. This is the famously haunted landscape of Kenidjack Carn, which local superstition identified as the playground of giants and devils. From the high ground the linear pattern of Pendeen's mining coast is spread out before you with the glittering Atlantic beyond. The walk then leads back towards Pendeen and past the Church of St John, built by the mining community in the 1850s using rock quarried from the hilltop of Carn Eanes.

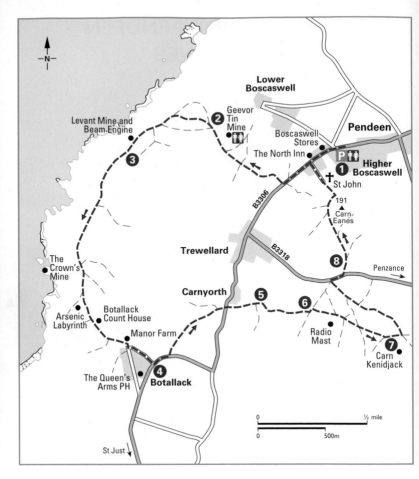

1. Turn left out of the car park and follow the road around to the entrance of the Geevor Tin Mine. Go down the drive towards the reception building and when you reach it keep to its left, between it and the shop and café building. When you come to it go through a gap and follow a road along between buildings.

2. Opposite the last buildings, turn left to walk along a track, signposted 'Levant', by some large boulders. Follow the path towards three tall chimney stacks ahead. Ignoring a track that heads left by a very large rock, go left at a fork, then straight over a broad stony track to reach Levant Mine and Beam Engine on your right.

3. Pass the bottom end of Levant car park and follow a rough track, keeping left early on where it divides into three, to go past Roscommon Cottage to reach the Botallack Count House. (The Queen's Arms pub is straight down the road directly opposite Manor Farm.) Keep on past Manor Farm and reach the public road at Botallack.

4. Turn left, then left again at the main road (watch for fast traffic), then turn left at the Cresswell Terrace sign to a stile. Follow field paths to Carnyorth.

Cross the main road, then follow the lane opposite, past a row of cottages, to reach a solitary house.

5. Keep left of the house and then go over a stile and go diagonally across the field to the opposite hedge to reach a hidden stile. Follow a path through small fields towards a radio mast. Cross a final stile on to a rough track.

6. Go left, then immediately right at a junction. Keep on past the radio mast, then follow a path through gorse and heather to the rocky outcrop of Carn Kenidjack (not always visible when misty).

7. At a junction abreast of Carn Kenidjack, go left along a path past a small granite parish boundary stone, eventually reaching a gate, beyond which is a path through scrub and finally a road. Turn right and in about 140yds (128m), go left along an obvious broad track opposite a house.

8. Keep left at a junction and then straight ahead at the next junction. When abreast of two large rocks on the left, go right between two smaller stone pillars and through a wooden gate. Keep straight ahead across rough ground and then go alongside an overgrown wall. Go left over a big stone stile directly above the church and descend to the main road. Turn right to the car park.

Where to eat and drink
Halfway along the route is The Queen's Arms in Botallack village; pub meals are available. The North Inn at Pendeen is another traditional inn, and Heather's Coffee Shop is a pleasant place at the end of the walk as you come down the lane from the church. There is a café at Geevor Tin Mine.

What to see
Just below the track that runs past the Botallack Count House lie the ruins of an arsenic labyrinth. Mineral ore was often contaminated with arsenic. In the 19th century during times of low tin prices, this arsenic was collected by roasting ore in a calciner and passing the smoke through enclosed tunnels, the labyrinth. The cooling vapour deposited the arsenic on the labyrinth walls as a powder that was then exported, mainly to America as a pesticide against the boll weevil in the cotton fields. Its effect on both the labyrinth workers and the field workers does not bear thinking about.

While you're there
A visit to the Geevor Tin Mine is worthwhile for the background to the history of Cornish mineral mining. Part of the experience is an underground tour and a visit to the old treatment sheds. The National Trust's restored engine house at Levant Mine and Beam Engine contains a remarkable reconstruction of a fully operative Cornish beam engine, the great driving force of every Victorian mine.

23 ST JUST AND CAPE CORNWALL

DISTANCE/TIME	6.5 miles (5.5km) / 2hrs
ASCENT/GRADIENT	262ft (80m) / ▲ ▲ ▲
PATHS	Mostly well defined; some coastal sections steep and rocky; may be wet and muddy; many stiles
LANDSCAPE	Coastal area with industrial archaeology
SUGGESTED MAP	AA Walker's Map 10 Land's End & The Lizard
START/FINISH	Grid reference: SW369313
DOG FRIENDLINESS	Lead required in field sections where there may be livestock
PARKING	St Just free car park, opposite the library
PUBLIC TOILETS	St Just car park and Cape Cornwall car park
NOTES	The walk can be started either from St Just car park or alternatively from the National Trust car park at Cape Cornwall (Point 6), where there is a fee for non-National Trust members

St Just is the most westerly town in England, and Cape Cornwall is the only Cape in England. Both were once at the heart of Cornwall's mining industry. Mining has now ceased, but the history of St Just is of such significance that the area is now a part of the Devon and Cornwall World Heritage Mining Site.

The cliffs of Cape Cornwall are not composed of the golden granite typical of the Land's End Peninsula. They comprise more ancient rocks, known as 'country rock' – the primeval sedimentary shales that were later transformed and 'baked' by the molten granite that erupted from deep within the earth. The intense heat, chemical reactions and physical changes that took place produced the abundant mineral deposits that made west Cornwall famous. During the heyday of Victorian mining, this area was a vibrant, if bleak, industrial landscape with more than 2,000 people employed in mining. Today, what survives are the granite chimney stacks, buildings, wheel pits and water leats of the mine processing works that once filled the valleys and cliffside with sound and fury and swirling clouds of smoke and dust.

Amid all of this, men, women and children worked endlessly in one of the toughest environments ever. We marvel at the romance of it all, but the reality was often brutal. Mineral ores were rich in arsenic, and the 'calciner' building passed on this walk was used to extract arsenic from raw ore at times when tin was unprofitable. Arsenic commanded good prices as a pesticide. The ore was 'baked' in the calciners, and the smoke drafted through labyrinthine tunnels. The arsenic was deposited as powder on the tunnel walls and was then scraped off, mainly by women and young boys whose lungs and skin were unprotected. Life expectancy for the arsenic harvesters was low. The ruins around Cape Cornwall serve as memorials to a dramatic industry and to a remarkable people.

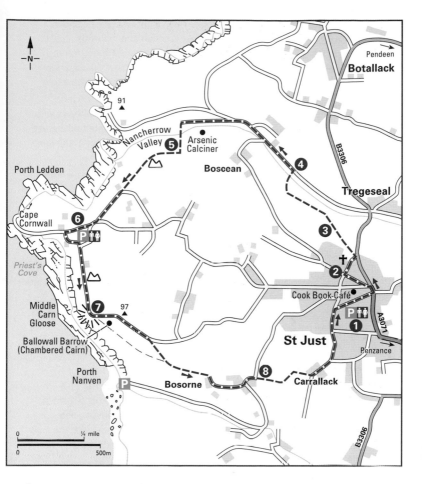

1. Leave the car park and turn right to reach Market Square. Turn left, and at a road junction beside a clock tower go straight across (with care) and down the narrow Chapel Street.

2. At a T-junction, with the Wesleyan chapel opposite, turn right. At a junction with the main road, by a public footpath sign, go left along a narrow passageway in front of two cottages. Go over a stile and cross a small field to another stile. Go diagonally right across the next field towards three telegraph poles.

3. Go over a stile, then bear round left and alongside the field-edge to another stile. Follow the path between trees, then go over a stile and cross a road at a waste water plant. Go over a stile and a footbridge to a surfaced lane.

4. Turn left along the lane. Keep ahead onto a rough track at a junction by a house. At the next junction keep right along the track, and at the next junction, by a National Trust sign for Kenidjack, take the left-hand branch downhill, forking left beside extensive mine ruins. Turn left at Coast Path signs along a narrow path and across a footbridge.

5. Follow the path as it winds steeply uphill. Keep right where it begins to level off at a T-junction. Keep right at the next junction and follow the coast path. Turn right at a junction and pass above a whitewashed house to reach a surfaced road above Cape Cornwall. Two paces before the road, turn right along the coast path then head out onto the road opposite the entrance to a National Trust car park.

6. Turn right along the road past the toilets. Turn sharp left at a gateway with a 'Private Road' sign, and go down a series of granite steps. Turn left up a steep surfaced lane at a junction above Priest's Cove. Turn sharply right at the next junction and follow a stony track uphill to Middle Carn Gloose.

7. Follow a surfaced road past the Ballowall Barrow Bronze Age grave. Turn right down a track about 150yds (137m) beyond a mine stack and opposite a bench. Keep straight ahead across two junctions to a surfaced road that leads between houses. Keep left at a broad junction and go up the lane opposite for 100yds (90m).

8. Turn right in front of a house called Porth Nanven Barn and go through a gate and then a kissing gate. Follow a path that becomes overgrown to a stile. Cross a field to a step stile by a tall wooden post. Turn left along the field-edge. Go over a stile at buildings to reach a lane. Turn left and carry straight on, ignoring three roads leading off to the right. Take the fourth, Market Street, to return to the car park, which is now in sight.

Where to eat and drink

The Cook Book Café at 4 Cape Cornwall Street is just down from the clock tower in St Just, and should not be missed, if only for its terrific collection of over 5,000 second-hand books, with many gems among them. The food is excellent also. Enjoy fresh mackerel, smoked on the premises, delicious soups, baguettes, homemade cakes and much more. There are also several pubs in St Just serving bar food.

What to see

Cape Cornwall was once noted for growing peaches, melons and grapes. This was the work of a remarkable local mining engineer, Francis Oats, who worked in South Africa and became the chairman of Cecil Rhodes' De Beers Company in 1908. Oats built the imposing Porthledden House, the 'baronial'-looking mansion above the Cape. He also built huge greenhouses at the Cape in which exotic fruits were cultivated. You can spot the foundations of the greenhouses, seaward of the granite steps at waypoint 6.

While you're there

The latter part of the walk takes you past the striking ancient monument of Ballowall Barrow. Now in the care of the National Trust, this dramatic monument dates from about 2000 BC and is a middle Bronze Age entrance grave. The site was once obscured by a large dump of mine waste, and ultimately may owe its preservation and survival to this.

ST JUST TO LAND'S END

DISTANCE/TIME	6.5 miles (10.4km) / 3hrs 30min
ASCENT/GRADIENT	328ft (100m) / ▲
PATHS	Good coastal footpaths; can be rocky in places
LANDSCAPE	West-facing coast with low cliffs and golden beach
SUGGESTED MAP	AA Walker's Map 10 Land's End & The Lizard
START	Grid reference: SW369314
FINISH	Grid reference: SW344250
DOG FRIENDLINESS	Dogs on lead through grazed areas and as notices indicate
PARKING	St Just main car park on Market Street, opposite St Just Library; large free car park
PUBLIC TOILETS	St Just free car park; Sennen; Land's End
NOTES	Buses run between Land's End and St Just several times a day, May–October. For more information visit www.travelinesw.com

By way of taking the long view towards Land's End, this walk follows footpaths from the old mining town of St Just and then along an exhilarating stretch of coast that runs south to Sennen Cove and to Land's End.

St Just is an attractive town of sturdy granite houses surrounding a central market square. There was probably some kind of settlement at St Just in prehistoric times, but the town became an important centre of tin and copper mining, especially during the 18th and 19th centuries, and although the last mine in the area closed during the 1990s, St Just has not lost its traditional character. To the immediate west of the town is Cape Cornwall, a shapely promontory that could vie with Land's End for scenic impact. The coast to either side of the Cape is a treasure-house of mining history and today, at nearby Geevor Mine, this great Cornish industry is celebrated at a splendid museum among the dramatic relics of the past.

The first part of this walk reaches the coast at Porth Nanven, via Cot Valley, one of the earliest areas of mineral mining in west Cornwall. From here the coastal footpath is followed south. To the left of the first section of the path are the gaping vents of old mining 'adits', tunnels into the cliff face created by early miners excavating veins of rich ore. (Don't be tempted to explore any yourself; they can be dangerously unstable.) Offshore lie the rocky islands of the Brisons, said to have once served as a castaway prison for criminals. The path soon leaves the more obvious mining area and follows the delightful shoreline towards Land's End, dropping to sea level as it reaches the great beaches of Whitesand Bay and the granite cliffs of the Land's End area. The beaches here are some of Cornwall's finest surfing venues. Beyond Sennen's charming seafront, the path climbs once more and soon reaches Land's End.

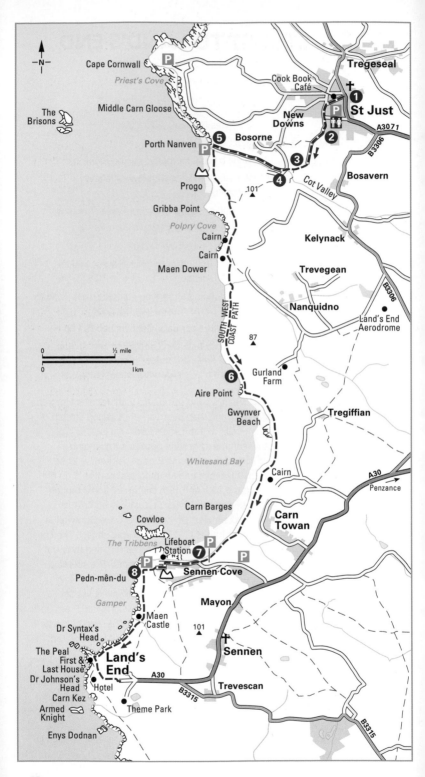

1. From Market Square in St Just, go down Market Street, to the right of the Commercial Hotel and past the free car park and library. At a T-junction, turn left and follow Bosorne Terrace, keeping straight ahead at a junction.

2. Where the road curves left at another junction, keep to the right and follow a narrow lane, for 0.25 miles (400m) to where the lane ends by a seat. Go right from here and follow a hedged-in track.

3. At a junction, just beyond a granite pillar, go left and downhill past Brook Cottage, then turn right down the stone steps and follow an enclosed path across a stream to reach a junction with a surfaced track. Turn right here, then left on a lane to reach a junction with a surfaced road by Cot Valley Cottage.

4. Turn left and follow the road down the narrow Cot Valley, for 0.5 miles (0.8km) to reach a parking area at Porth Nanven. You can view the raised beach (see What to see) by continuing along a path towards the sea.

5. From Porth Nanven, take the coast path across the stream and climb steeply uphill. For the next 1.5 miles (2.4km) the path rises past boulder-crammed beaches and crumbling cliffs, then descends almost to sea level.

6. Keep along the coast path, up steps and past the rocky outcrop of Aire Point. Continue above the famous surfing beach of Gwynver. On approaching Sennen Beach, pass in front of two wooden chalets. Go ahead and then between a dark grey cottage and one called Basking Shark. Continue up the sandy path, zig-zagging steeply upwards to the car park at the entrance to Sennen Beach.

7. Leave by the car park entrance and keep ahead along the seafront walkway through Sennen Cove. Reach the Cove's lifeboat house and beyond this, the Capstan Gallery. Continue to a car park. Go through the car park, then go left up steepish steps and a pathway to reach the top of the rocky headland of Pedn-Mên-Du, where the National Trust has a seasonal information point in the old coastguard lookout.

8. From the old coastguard lookout, follow the coastal footpath along the edge of spectacular cliffs for just under 1 mile (1.6km) to reach the First and Last House. Continue to the Land's End Hotel and the unbeatable views.

Where to eat and drink

St Just has a number of pubs and cafés. The Cook Book Café in Cape Cornwall Street is a delight. The Surf Beach Bar, which serves pizzas and burgers, overlooks Sennen Beach. There's a pub, the Old Success, and cafés in Sennen Cove. Land's End has a pub and other outlets.

What to see

The section of coast from Porth Nanven to Aire Point has some remarkable examples of raised beach. These are sections of wave-cut platforms that are now above sea level.

While you're there

St Just was once at the heart of Cornish coastal mining and is an attractive town to explore.

FROM PORTHCURNO TO MINACK

DISTANCE/TIME	3.5 miles (5.7km) / 2hrs 30min
ASCENT/GRADIENT	164ft (50m) / ▲ ▲
PATHS	Coastal footpaths
LANDSCAPE	Granite sea cliffs and inland fields and heath
SUGGESTED MAP	AA Walker's Map 10 Land's End & The Lizard
START/FINISH	Grid reference: SW384224
DOG FRIENDLINESS	Dogs should be kept under control on beach and fields, and under close control on cliff tops from March to July to avoid disturbing nesting Cornish choughs
PARKING	Porthcurno; St Levan; Porthgwarra
PUBLIC TOILETS	Porthgwarra and Porthcurno

For the true aficionado of coastal scenery, the granite cliffs of Porthcurno and Porthgwarra are hard to beat. Gwennap Head, at Porthgwarra, is the most southerly point on the Land's End Peninsula. The Atlantic tidal flow divides at the base of Gwennap's spectacular Chair Ladder cliff, one flow running eastwards up the English Channel, the other running north, up St George's Channel between Britain and Ireland.

This walk starts at Porthcurno, where a sweeping expanse of almost white shell sand lies at the heart of an arc of golden granite cliffs that embrace the small bay. On the south side lies the rocky coxcomb of Treryn Dinas, or Logan Rock. To the north is the famous Minack Theatre, built within the rocky ribs of the headland. The final section of the walk passes the Minack, but first the route leads inland and across fields to the splendid little church of St Levan, couched in one of the few sheltered spots on this robust coast. Below the church, a shallow valley runs down to Porth Chapel Beach, more besieged by tides than Porthcurno, but still a delightful place, especially in summer. Again the beach here is left for later in the walk, whose route now leads along the coast path and then climbs inland before dropping down to Porthgwarra Cove, where tunnels and caverns in the cliff were carved out by farmers and fishermen to give better access to the narrow beach. From Porthgwarra, you head back along the coast path to Porth Chapel (for a visit to Gwennap Head). The path leads you down past the little Well of St Levan. Below here there is a rocky access path to the beach.

The route of the walk leads steeply up to Rospletha Point and then to the remarkable cliff-face theatre at Minack (see What to see). From here, the most direct way down to Porthcurno Beach is by a series of very steep steps that may not suit everyone. But if you don't mind the vertiginous experience, the views really are outstanding. You can avoid this descent by some judicious road walking. Either way, Porthcurno's glorious beach is at hand in the cove below you.

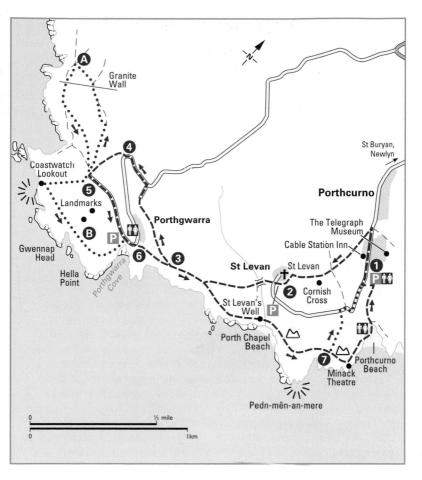

1. From Porthcurno car park, walk back up the approach road, then just before Sea View House, turn sharply left along a track and follow it to reach cottages. Keep around to the front of the cottages. Go through a wide gateway in the wall opposite, then follow a path through the middle of a field past a granite cross and through a wooden gate.

2. Enter St Levan churchyard by a granite stile. Go round the far side of the church to the entrance gate and on to a surfaced lane. Cross the lane and follow the path opposite, signed to Porthgwarra. Cross a footbridge, then in about 55yds (50m), at a junction, take the right fork and follow the path across a field to merge with the main coast path, and keep ahead.

3. Where the path begins to descend towards Porthgwarra Cove, branch off right up five wooden steps. Reach a surfaced track by a house and turn up right, then at a road, turn left.

4. Go round a sharp left-hand bend, then at a footpath signpost, go right down a grassy path and cross a stone footbridge. Continue uphill to reach a bend on a track, just up from large granite houses.

5. Turn left, go over a stile beside a gate, then continue down a surfaced lane to Porthgwarra Cove. Just past the shop and café, opposite a phone box, go right down a track signposted 'Coast Path', then follow the path round to the left. Just past a house, go sharp right at the junction and climb up the steps.

6. Continue along the coast path, partly reversing the previous route past waypoint 3. Keep right at a junction, and eventually descend past St Levan's Well to just above Porth Chapel Beach. (Dogs should be on a lead.) Follow the coast path steeply over Pedn-mên-an-mere, and continue on the coast path to the Minack Theatre car park.

7. For the surefooted, cross the car park and go down the track to the left of the Minack complex, then descend the steep cliff steps, with great care. When the path levels off, continue to a junction. The right fork takes you to Porthcurno Beach and back to the car park. A less challenging alternative to the cliff steps is to turn left out of the Minack car park. Follow the approach road to a T-junction with a public road. Turn right, watching out for traffic.

Extending the walk You can extend the main walk by following the coast path across Gwennap Head to the west of Porthgwarra Cove. At waypoint 5 on the main walk turn right off the surfaced track and go along a grassy track. In 30yds (27m), where the track forks, take the right fork and follow a grassy track across the open heathland, a glorious mosaic of purple heather and golden gorse in late summer. Keep left at the next fork and soon pass through a gap in a granite wall. A few paces beyond the wall, take the far left fork. Keep ahead along the track to reach the coast path, Point A, by an old tyre capstan. Turn left here along a short path and in a few steps merge with the coast path. Go through a kissing gate in the granite wall ahead and keep left at forks to descend gently to the bend in the track by waypoint 5 once more. Turn right up the road that leads to the National Coastwatch lookout, and turn left along the coast path. Follow the path past two incongruous, brightly painted concrete cones protruding from the heather, Point B. They are landmarks to assist mariners in fixing the position of the dangerous Runnelstone Reef. Follow the coast path all the way round Hella Point to reach the surfaced road above Porthgwarra Cove, where you rejoin the main walk at waypoint 6.

Where to eat and drink
There is a seasonal café at Porthgwarra. Porthcurno has several outlets including the Beach Café and the Cable Station Inn. A seasonal ice cream and soft drinks outlet is in the Porthcurno car park.

What to see
The Minack Theatre was the unusual creation of Rowena Cade, whose family bought the rocky headland in the 1920s. Today performances of a variety of plays and musicals are staged during the summer months.

While you're there
The Telegraph Museum at Porthcurno, located above the top end of the car park, deserves a visit.

ALONG THE COAST FROM LAMORNA COVE

DISTANCE/TIME	6 miles (9.7km) / 3hrs 30min
ASCENT/GRADIENT	558ft (170m) / ▲ ▲
PATHS	Coastal footpaths (can be rocky and close to cliff edge in places) and field paths, several stiles
LANDSCAPE	Picturesque coastline, fields and wooded valleys
SUGGESTED MAP	AA Walker's Map 10 Land's End & The Lizard
START/FINISH	Grid reference: SW450241
DOG FRIENDLINESS	Dogs on lead through grazed areas
PARKING	Lamorna Cove (fee-paying car park); Boskenna Cross (lay-by)
PUBLIC TOILETS	None on the route

The coast at Lamorna, to the southwest of Penzance, is one of the loveliest in Cornwall. This is a south-facing coast, protected from prevailing westerly winds although storms from the south and east can be merciless here, as witnessed by a record of terrible shipwrecks over the years. The bare granite cliffs are enhanced by swathes of lush vegetation that turn the coast into something of a wild garden in spring and summer.

The walk starts from Lamorna Cove, once the scene of granite quarrying. The quay at Lamorna was built so that ships could load up with the quarried stone, but the swell and the tides made berthing difficult. Much of the stone was carried overland by horse and wagon to Newlyn Harbour and to Penzance. The coast path west from Lamorna winds through tumbled granite boulders, then climbs steeply to the cliff tops. It passes above Tater-du Lighthouse, by jet-black greenstone cliffs, startling among miles of golden granite, although the upper parts of the greenstone are dusted with ochre-coloured lichen.

Soon the path descends steeply to the delightful St Loy's Cove, a secluded boulder beach where a brisk little stream pours out of a wooded valley. Spring comes early at St Loy: the subtropical vegetation through which the walk leads reflects the area's mild and moist microclimate. From St Loy's woods you climb inland to reach two enthralling ancient monuments. The first is the Tregiffian burial chamber, a late Bronze Age entrance grave that was uncovered during road widening in the 1960s. Just along the road from Tregiffian stands one of Cornwall's most famous monuments, the Merry Maidens stone circle. This late neolithic/Bronze Age structure represents an ancient ceremonial site of major importance. Its popular name, appended by a much later superstitious society, refers to a myth of young girls being turned to stone for dancing on a Sunday. In a field on the other side of the B3315 are two tall standing stones, the mythical 'Pipers' who supplied the sacrilegious music. The true spirit of the stones reflects a far more intriguing ancient culture. The final part of the walk leads from the Merry Maidens to a wonderful old trackway that leads over water-worn stones into the Lamorna Valley.

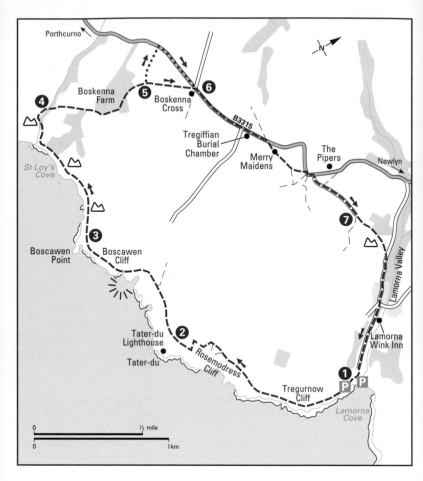

1. From the far end of the seaward car park in the cove, above Lamorna Harbour, follow the coast path through some awkward rocky sections. Continue along the coast path past the tops of Tregurnow Cliff and Rosemodress Cliff, bearing right at a fork along the way to stay on the coast path.

2. Pass above the entrance ramp and steps of Tater-du Lighthouse. Pass a row of residences on the right and then, where the track bends right, keep left along the narrow coast path, at a signpost.

3. Descend steeply (take great care when the ground is muddy) from Boscawen Cliff to St Loy's Cove. Cross over a section of sea-smoothed boulders that may be slippery when wet. Mid-way along the beach, follow a path inland through trees and alongside the stream. Cross a private drive and then climb steeply uphill. Turn sharp right over a stile and follow the path through trees.

4. By a wooden signpost and a sycamore, go down right and cross the stream on large boulders, then go left along a hedged-in path. In about 125yds (114m), go sharp right up a tiny unsigned path between a large tree and a rock and up to a surfaced lane. Follow the lane uphill. At a junction with another track, keep ahead and uphill. At Boskenna Farm buildings follow the surfaced lane round left and keep ahead.

5. From the lane, just past the entrance drive to a bungalow on the right, the right of way goes through a small metal gate next to a field gate. It then goes diagonally right and through a gap in a wire fence. Beyond this, the way (there's no path) leads diagonally across the field to its top right-hand corner, where a very high and awkward stile to the right of a makeshift five-bar gate leads into a large roadside lay-by with a granite cross at its edge. An alternative to the field route is to continue from the bungalow entrance along the farm lane, and then to turn right along the public road, with care, to reach the lay-by.

6. Go right and follow the road to the Tregiffian burial chamber on the right and then to the Merry Maidens stone circle. From the stone circle, follow a grassy path towards a gate in the field corner. Go over a steep stile on the left, then continue diagonally across the field, past a telegraph pole. Go through a small metal gate and descend rocky steps to a main road (watch out for traffic). Turn right and follow the surfaced left-hand lane of two, signed 'Tregurnow Farm'.

7. Where the lane ends keep ahead on to a public bridleway. Follow a shady track downhill to reach Lamorna Valley. Turn right and walk down the road, with care, passing the Lamorna Wink Inn, to the car park.

Where to eat and drink

There's a shop and café at Lamorna Cove. The Lamorna Wink Inn serves bar meals and a wide range of specials, including several fish dishes. There are no food outlets on the route of the walk itself, but there are numerous delightful picnic spots on the coastal section.

What to see

If you do this walk in spring you will be treated to a genuine 'host of golden daffodils'. The cliffside paths are flanked by hundreds of daffodils that have spread from cultivated meadows. Another marvellous floral display is offered by the swathes of bluebells, found on the open cliffs and in the lush woodland behind St Loy's Cove.

While you're there

Spend some time at St Loy's Beach, often claimed as one of the first places in Britain to enjoy rising spring temperatures. There's not a grain of sand but the boulder beach with its little tidal channels is a delight on a peaceful summer's day, although in southeast storms the conditions here can be frightening. Just east of St Loy's Beach at Boscawen Point, in a ferocious storm in December 1981, the locally based lifeboat the *Solomon Browne* was lost with all eight of its crew. The lifeboatmen had made heroic efforts to save eight people, who also died, from the stricken vessel *Union Star*.

PRUSSIA COVE AND MOUNT'S BAY

DISTANCE/TIME	4 miles (6.4km) / 3hrs
ASCENT/GRADIENT	394ft (120m) / ▲ ▲
PATHS	Good field paths and coastal paths, many stiles
LANDSCAPE	Quiet coast and countryside
SUGGESTED MAP	AA Walker's Map 10 Land's End & The Lizard
START/FINISH	Grid reference: SW554282
DOG FRIENDLINESS	Dogs on lead through grazed areas
PARKING	Trenalls, Prussia Cove, small, privately owned car park. Or car park at Perranuthnoe, from where the walk can be started at waypoint 5
PUBLIC TOILETS	Perranuthnoe

Smuggling clings to the image of Cornwall like the Atlantic mist through which the old-time 'freetraders' so often stole ashore with their cargoes of tea, spirits, tobacco, silk, china and even playing cards. Modern smuggling, chiefly of drugs, has no such romantic sheen, but nostalgia blurs the record of incidental brutality that often accompanied 18th-century smuggling.

Such 'honest adventuring' seems personified by the famous Carter family, who lived at Prussia Cove on the eastern shores of Mount's Bay in west Cornwall. The cove is really more of a series of rocky inlets close to the magnificent St Michael's Mount, the castle-crowned island that so enhances the inner corner of Mount's Bay. John and Henry (Harry) Carter were the best known members of the family and ran their late 18th-century smuggling enterprise with great flair and efficiency. They even fortified the headland overlooking Prussia Cove in a move that echoed the defensive settlements of the Celtic Iron Age. John Carter was the more flamboyant, styling himself in early childhood games as 'the King of Prussia'. The name stuck and the original Porth Leah Cove became known as the 'King of Prussia's Cove'. He also had integrity. He once broke into an excise store in Penzance to recover smuggled goods confiscated from Prussia Cove in his absence. The authorities knew it must have been Carter because they said he was 'an upright man' and took only his own goods. His brother Harry became a Methodist preacher, and forbade swearing on all his vessels.

The remote nature of the coast and countryside around Prussia Cove says much about the environment in which smuggling flourished. As you follow the route of the walk, you can sense the remoteness, the secretiveness of the lanes and paths that wriggle inland from a coast that is formidable, yet accessible to skilled seamen. At Perranuthnoe, the narrow, flat beach resounds with the sound of the sea where modern surfers and holidaymakers now enjoy themselves. From here the coastal footpath leads back along the coast across the rocky headland of Cudden Point, to where a series of secluded inlets make up the Carters' old kingdom of Prussia Cove.

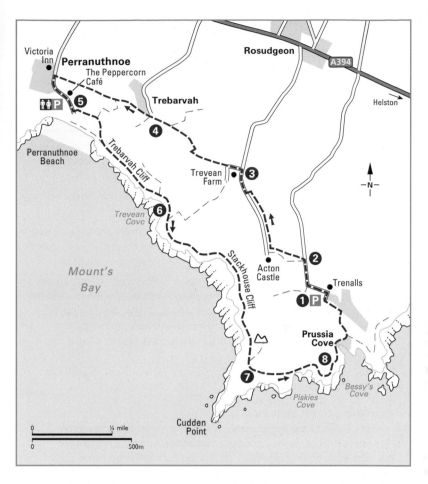

1. From the Trenells car park entrance walk back along the approach road, past the large house. Keep left and round the next sharp right-hand bend. Watch out for traffic. Ignore the first footpath sign on the left and, in about 150yds (138m), just past a wide gateway, go over a stile on the left, and into a field.

2. Follow the field-edge, bearing off to the right, where it bends around to the left, to reach a slate stile by a telegraph pole in the hedge opposite. Walk down the edge of the next field, behind the privately owned Acton Castle. Turn right and follow the bottom field-edge to its end. Go over a stile and follow the next field-edge to a gateway. Go through this and turn right along a lane.

3. On reaching tarmac, turn left along a rough track at a junction in front of a bungalow entrance at Trevean Farm. In 55yds (50m), by Trevean House, keep right, up a stony track, then go through a gate on the right, by Beare's Den campsite. Follow the left-hand edge of a long field to a stile on its top edge, then follow the right-hand edge of the next field.

4. At Trebarvah go through a kissing gate. Cross a lane and continue across a stony area with houses on your right (there's a view of St Michael's Mount ahead), then follow a field-edge to a hedged-in path. Keep ahead at a path junction and then go through fields and pass the front of houses to reach the road opposite the Victoria Inn. Go left and follow the road to the car park above Perranuthnoe Beach.

5. For the beach keep straight ahead. On the main route of the walk, go left, just beyond the car park, and along a surfaced lane. Bear right at a fork, then bear right again just past a house at a junction. Go down a rough track towards the sea and follow it round to the left. Then, at a field entrance, descend right (signposted), turn sharp left through a gap and follow the coast path.

6. At a junction above Trevean Cove, bear off right from the track to walk along a path that follows the cliff edge.

7. At the National Trust property of Cudden Point, ignore the broad inland path to your left and continue ahead around the coast. Then cross the inner slope of the headland above Piskies Cove, keeping right wherever the path divides.

8. Go through a gateway and pass some ancient fishing huts. Follow the path round the edge of the Bessy's Cove inlet of Prussia Cove. Turn left at a fork to go up some steps and reach a track by a thatched cottage. The cove can be reached down a path on the right just before this junction. Turn right and follow the track, past a post box. Keep left at junctions, to return to the car park at the start of the walk.

Where to eat and drink
The Victoria Inn at Perranuthnoe is conveniently located mid-way on the walk. The pub has a good selection of beers and other drinks and also does excellent bar meals. On the approach to Perranuthnoe Beach and before the car park is The Peppercorn Café, where the food is creative and delicious.

What to see
Along the sandy paths and fields east of Perranuthnoe, the feathery-leafed tamarisk (*Tamarix anglica*), lends a Mediterranean atmosphere to the Cornish scene. The tamarisk was introduced to Britain from the Mediterranean and is often used at coastal locations as a windbreak because of its resilience.

While you're there
Take time mid-way in the walk to enjoy Perranuthnoe Beach, known as Perran Sands, a fine little beach that is south-facing and catches the sun all day. It's also worth exploring Prussia Cove itself, and its individual rocky inlets. This is a good place for a swim at low tide in the crystal-clear water.

FROM HELSTON TO PORTHLEVEN BY THE LOE

DISTANCE/TIME	4 miles (6.4km) / 2hrs
ASCENT/GRADIENT	475ft (145m) / ▲
PATHS	Excellent paths and estate tracks
LANDSCAPE	Densely vegetated river valley, poolside woods and open farmland
SUGGESTED MAP	AA Walker's Map 10 Land's End & The Lizard
START	Grid reference: SW656272
FINISH	Grid reference: SW628257
DOG FRIENDLINESS	Dogs strictly on the lead within Penrose Park area; dogs banned on Porthleven Beach Easter to 1 October, from the Harbour Wall to the Blue Buoy steps. Rest of Porthleven has no restrictions
PARKING	Penrose Amenity Area free car park, Helston. Turn off the A394 on to the B3304 at the large roundabout on the outskirts of Helston. Car park is 200yds (183m) along the road on the left
PUBLIC TOILETS	Porthleven
NOTES	Buses 2, 2A, 2B Porthleven–Helston, about 20 per day; www.travelinesw.com

This undemanding walk leads from the attractive town of Helston to the fishing village of Porthleven, via the valley of the River Cober and the remarkable Loe, the largest natural freshwater lake in Cornwall. Helston has a rich Cornish identity and is worth exploring, not least for the fine Victorian and Edwardian architecture of Cross Street and Church Street to the north of the main road, and Coinagehall Street. The name of the latter is a clue to Helston's history from when it was a Stannary town where ingots of tin were checked for their quality by having a small corner, or *coign*, cut from them. Helston is also famous for its annual 'Furry Dance', staged in early May and known also as the Helston Flora. The main feature of the day is a series of processional dances in which women wear brightly patterned dresses and splendid bonnets, while men wear morning coats and top hats. The dancers pass through the main streets and also in and out of selected houses. This walk begins at the public car park beside the Penrose Amenity Area to the southwest of Helston. The route passes the ruin of the engine house of the old Castle Wary mine.

What makes the Loe exceptional is that its southern end is separated from the sea by a sand bar, known as Loe Bar. The Loe's name derives simply from the Cornish word *logh*, meaning 'pool'. The Loe evolved in medieval times from its origins as the estuary of the River Cober because of a build-up of silt washed down from the countless tin and copper mines inland. The silt added its weight to encroaching shingle spits at the seaward end of the estuary and by the 13th century, a formidable dam, or 'bar', of sand and shingle separated the pool from the sea. Until the middle of the 19th century Loe Bar was regularly breached by gangs of diggers to ease flooding in the Cober Valley below Helston. The rush of water out of the pool is said to have left a thin yellow stain for miles offshore. Today, modern flood release systems alleviate the problem of flooding and the Loe has become a splendid reserve for wildlife.

The Loe lies within the Penrose Estate, ancestral home of the Penrose family and then the Rogers family, who gave the estate to the National Trust in 1974. The Trust now maintains the landscaping and carriageways and has created a network of public paths. The latter part of the walk follows the coast to Porthleven, a classic Cornish fishing village with a fine harbour.

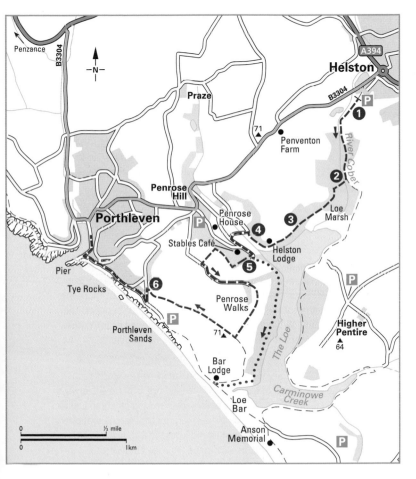

1. Start from the large car park on the B3304 Porthleven road just outside Helston. At the far, southern, end of the car park go through a gap to the left of the 'Penrose Amenity Area' sign and then turn right along a concrete drive, past a National Trust sign, 'Penrose'. In about 0.5 miles (800m) pass an old chimney stack, the remains of the 18th-century Castle Wary lead and silver mine.

2. In a few yards, turn right down some steps, cross a bridge over the River Cober and continue ahead across a sturdy causeway that was built in 1987. Dogs must be kept on the lead here. You are now at the heart of Loe Marsh, the choked gut of the River Cober, dense with alder and willow trees and moisture-loving plants. On the other side of the causeway, turn left along a wide drive through the Oak Grove.

3. In about 550yds (500m) look for a short path on the left. It leads to a bird hide in a fine location for viewing the reedy shores of the Loe. Continue along the main drive to Helston Lodge, go through a gate, and then follow the drive to where it forks.

4. Take the left fork. There is a fine view of Penrose House from here; the house is a private dwelling. Continue past the old stable block, now a National Trust café and offices. Due to a major landslip, the path that follows the shore of the Loe along an old carriageway through Bar Walk Plantation to Bar Lodge above Loe Bar is closed at time of going to print. An alternative coastal route is being planned.

5. In the meantime, follow the diversion to the right soon after passing the Stables Café. Continue along this broad track over the gentle rises and farmland of the Penrose Estate following the clear diversions signs to Porthleven, enjoying fine views of the Loe below. The section of the route from here to Loe Bar is still open, so for a longer walk it's still possible to visit the sandbar and return to waypoint 5 to continue onwards to Porthleven.

6. On the main route, turn left when the diversion signs eventually lead you to a road. Then bear right at a hairpin bend to walk along the coast into Porthleven Harbour and village.

Where to eat and drink

Porthleven has several pubs, restaurants and cafés. The Nauti But Ice café serves ice creams and coffee. The Harbour Inn is a pub with a pleasing atmosphere, good food and a fine selection of beers. The National Trust-run Stables Café is beautifully situated near Penrose House around the halfway point of the walk.

What to see

The Loe is a sanctuary for birds including moorhen, mallard, teal and mute swan. Most of these are winter visitors, but there is always something to see. Ospreys have been known to stop off at the Loe for a taste of the lake's trout. Look for cormorants and herons that often perch in the Monterey pines just inland from the Bar. Aside from birds, there are many exotic shrubs within the Penrose Estate.

While you're there

Stroll across Loe Bar up to the Anson Memorial on its southeastern side. This simple stone cross commemorates the loss of the 44-gun frigate *Anson*, wrecked on Loe Bar in 1807. Over 100 sailors drowned, many of them as they tried to struggle ashore through the surf. Those on the beach could do nothing to save them.

MULLION COVE'S WILD FLOWERS

DISTANCE/TIME	7 miles (11.3km) / 4hrs
ASCENT/GRADIENT	978ft (298m) / ▲ ▲
PATHS	Good inland tracks and paths, can be muddy in places during wet weather. Coastal footpath, many stiles
LANDSCAPE	Flat heathland and high sea cliff
SUGGESTED MAP	AA Walker's Map 10 Land's End & The Lizard
START/FINISH	Grid reference: SW669162
DOG FRIENDLINESS	Dogs on lead through grazed areas and as notices indicate
PARKING	Predannack Wollas car park (National Trust)
PUBLIC TOILETS	Mullion Cove, 200yds (183m) up road from harbour

The heathland of the Lizard Peninsula near Mullion may seem dull compared to the dramatic sea cliffs that define its edges; the only punctuation marks are the huge satellite dishes of the nearby Goonhilly tracking station and the lazily revolving blades of modern wind turbines. Yet, beneath the skin, this seemingly featureless landscape is botanically unique and exciting, not least because the Lizard's calcareous soil is rich in magnesium and supports plants that are more often seen in chalk or limestone regions. The warming influence of the sea and the area's generally mild and frost-free climate encourages growth. The Lizard's most famous plant is the Cornish heath, rare in Britain generally, but abundant on the Lizard. In full bloom it contributes to a glorious mosaic of colour, its pink and white flowers matched by the brilliant yellow of western gorse and the deeper pinks of cross-leaved heath and bell heather. More common plants include spring squill, thrift and foxglove. Deeper into the heath are a variety of orchids including the rare green-winged orchid, with its purple-lipped flowers.

Near the turning point of the walk, the route joins the coast at Gew Graze, a feature that is also known as 'Soapy Cove' because of the presence of steatite, or soapstone. This is a fairly rare type of rock which was used in the 18th-century production of china and porcelain. The final part of the route, along the cliffs to Mullion Cove, brings more flower-spotting opportunities. On the path out of Gew Graze look for the yellow bracts and purple florets of carline thistle; the straw-coloured bracts curl over the flower heads to protect them in wet weather. Another remarkable plant is thyme broomrape, a dark reddish-brown, almost dead-looking plant that obtains its chlorophyll as a parasite growing on thyme. Such plants are often difficult to spot, whereas the smooth grassy slopes of the cliff tops near Mullion are a riot of blue spring squill, white sea campion and the yellow heads of lesser celandine and kidney vetch.

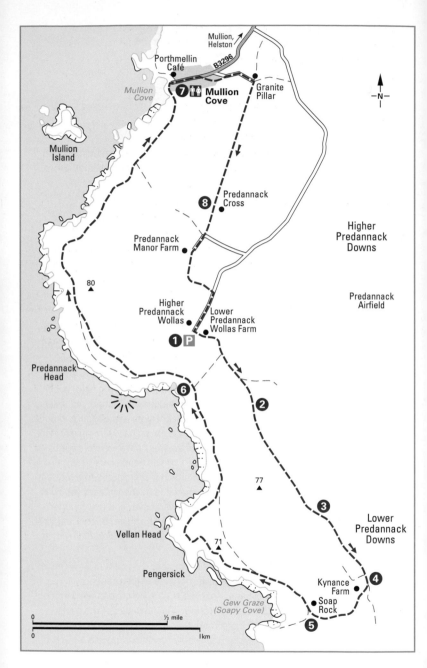

1. Leave the car park by its bottom end through a gate by the last house and follow the track ahead for 0.3 miles (0.5km). Ignore the signposted link to the coast path. Where the track bends to the left (signposted) continue on a secondary track directly ahead to reach a field gate in a few steps. Beyond the gate, keep straight ahead to go over a stile in the wall to your right, just

left of an opening into another field. Turn left along the field-edge. Cross another stile, then continue to open ground by a gate in a fence on the right.

2. Go over the wooden stile, then bear half left along a path to reach Natural England's National Nature Reserve. Keep ahead towards distant buildings. At a large field, keep along its left edge.

3. In approximately 150yds (137m), go left through a gap, signposted, then cross the field to reach a rough track. Turn right along the track for a few paces then go left through a gate and keep ahead along a path.

4. Go through a gate and then follow a track going right. Merge with another track, passing below a farmhouse, then in a few paces, and just before a ford, bear off to the right along a track towards the coast.

5. At an unsigned crossing with the coast path, go right and steeply uphill, then go over a stile on to the cliff top. Follow the coast path as it winds round the edge of the often projecting cliffs at Pengersick and Vellan Head.

6. Go left at a junction, just past a National Trust sign, 'Predannack'. (You can return to the car park by following the inland path from here.) Cross a stream in a dip and climb up left and continue round the cliff tops of Predannack Head. In about 1 mile (1.6km) arrive above Mullion Cove. (You can divert down left to visit Mullion Harbour, if desired.)

7. On the main route, turn right up the road and turn right at Mullion Mill Farm and some holiday cottages to follow a track. On a bend and just before a granite pillar, go right and over a stone stile into a field. Follow the path ahead through gorse and thorn trees and then through fields.

8. Pass close to a tall granite cross. Reach a lane by houses. Keep ahead along the lane towards Predannack Manor Farm. Just before the farm entrance, go left over a stile by a field gate, then follow the track along the edge of the field. Go over a stile by a barn, then left along a hedged-in path, cross a stile and cross two fields to reach a lane (watch out for traffic). Turn right to Predannack Wollas Farm car park.

Where to eat and drink
There is the rather good Porthmellin Café at Mullion Harbour, which serves all-day breakfasts, morning coffee, light lunches, cream teas, ice creams and soft drinks.

What to see
The Predannack Cross is a well-preserved Celtic cross. There was almost certainly a Celtic church in these parts too, evidence for which can be found in the local place-name Lanfrowder (a corruption of Lafrowda, the Kernowek name for St Just in Penwith).

While you're there
Spend some time at Mullion Harbour, dating from the 1890s and built like a fortress because the cove's position on the eastern shore of Mount's Bay leaves it open to the most ferocious storms from the west and southwest. This western coast of the Lizard Peninsula was always known as a 'wrecking shore', especially in the days of sail.

FROM LIZARD VILLAGE TO LIZARD POINT

DISTANCE/TIME	6.5 miles (10.4km) / 4hrs
ASCENT/GRADIENT	220ft (67m) / ▲ ▲ ▲
PATHS	Coastal footpaths, inland tracks and lanes. Please take note of path diversion notices at any erosion repair areas; several stiles
LANDSCAPE	Spectacular sea cliffs backed by open heathland
SUGGESTED MAP	AA Walker's Map 10 Land's End & The Lizard
START/FINISH	Grid reference: SW703125
DOG FRIENDLINESS	Dogs on lead through grazed areas
PARKING	Large car park at centre of Lizard village. Donation box. Can be busy in summer
PUBLIC TOILETS	By car park at Lizard village and at Kynance Cove

On the high ground of Lizard Point stands one of the most strategically important lighthouses in Britain. A coal-fired Lizard Lighthouse was built in 1619, but was short-lived, and it was not until 1752 that a more substantial lighthouse was built. It was first powered by coal and then, from 1812, by oil. Today's light is electric and has one of the most powerful beams in Britain.

The route of the walk first leads to the picturesque Kynance Cove, then on to Lizard Head and Lizard Point. In Polpeor Cove, on the western side of Lizard Point, stands the disused lifeboat house of the old Lizard lifeboat. This was a bold location; the launching slipway faced into the teeth of southerly and westerly gales and too often it was impossible to launch the lifeboat, though epic missions were carried out over the years. In 1961 the lifeboat house was closed on the opening of a new lifeboat station at the more sheltered Kilcobben Cove near Landewednack's Church Cove to the east. A new lifeboat house in a stylish modernist design was opened in 2012.

The Lizard was also famous for its connections with radio communications, a technology that has played its own crucial part in search and rescue at sea. East of Lizard Lighthouse, the route of the walk leads past the little wooden building of the old Marconi Wireless Station. From here, in 1901, the first wireless transmission was sent by Guglielmo Marconi. The letter 'S' in Morse code was sent from a now-demolished 164ft (50m) aerial. It was received faintly – but almost immediately – over 2,000 miles (3,240km) away at St John's, Newfoundland, where the aerial had been attached to a kite. Within sight of the 'Marconi Bungalow', as the little building is called, is the ugly, white-painted building of the old Lloyds signal station on Bass Point. The original station was established in 1872 to take note of all shipping that passed the Lizard. In front of the Lloyds building is a one-time coastguard lookout that is now manned by members of the National Coastwatch Institution. The new lifeboat station is just a little more than half a mile away.

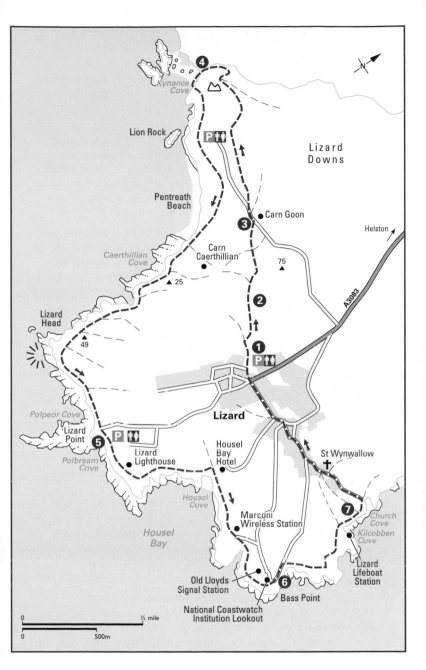

1. Turn right, when facing the public toilets at the bottom end of the car park, and go along a surfaced lane signed 'To Caerthillian and Kynance Coves'. In 80yds (70m) bear right at a junction and go along a track, signed 'Public Footpath Kynance Cove'. After 30yds (28m), at a public footpath sign, bear off left behind a chalet and go up some steps, then follow a path along the top of a broad stone wall (known as a 'hedge' in Cornwall).

2. Descend steps, keep right at a junction and then go through a privet grove. Negotiate two more sets of steps, then bear slightly right across a field. Go over a step stile to reach a road.

3. Follow the road ahead past the house, called Carn Goon. In a few paces bear away slightly right along a track. Reach a junction with a wide stony track at the bottom end of the National Trust car park for Kynance Cove. Turn right to take the track to Kynance Cove, arriving by the café.

4. Walk left along the beach and up the cliff steps and path to where a path goes off right, signed 'Coastal Path to Lizard Point'. Follow a cobbled and stepped path steeply uphill, then keep to the edge of the cliff along the coast path for about 1.25 miles (2km). Pass above Pentreath Beach and Caerthillian Cove and continue to rocky Lizard Head, then to Lizard Point and a car park and cafés.

5. Cross the car park and follow the coast path past the lighthouse. Look for access to the Lighthouse Visitor Centre (see While you're there). Descend steeply into Housel Cove and ascend just as steeply, ignoring a link path heading inland to Lizard village. Pass the old Marconi Wireless Station, now a small museum, the old Lloyds Signal Station and then the National Coastwatch Institution Lookout at Bass Point.

6. Follow a track past houses, then bear off right and follow the narrow coast path past Hot Point and on to the modern lifeboat house at Kilcobben Cove.

7. Go down steps on the far side of the lifeboat station and follow the coast path to Church Cove. Follow the public lane inland past St Wynwallow Church and continue uphill. Keep left at a junction to a second junction on a bend beside a granite cross and a seat. Go left along Beacon Terrace to the car park.

Where to eat and drink

At Lizard Point car park there are two cafés, with reduced hours in winter. Just off the coast path, on the east side of Housel Cove, is the Housel Bay Hotel where you can stop for a full meal. In the summer meals can be enjoyed on the summer terrace which overlooks the cliff-side gardens. Dogs are not allowed in the hotel restaurant. There's an open-air café at Kynance Cove. There are also several cafés and shops at Lizard village, as well as a fish and chip shop and a pub that serves meals. In Beacon Terrace is Ann's Pasties, a Cornish institution.

What to see

At Kynance Cove, look out for the delicate yellow petals of bird's-foot trefoil, which grows abundantly, flowering in July and August. More yellow adornments come in the form of the much rarer hairy greenweed, which only grows in west Cornwall and Wales. Watch out for pillows of bright yellow on rocky outcrops near waypoint 4.

While you're there

The Lizard Lighthouse has a visitor centre full of fascinating artefacts relating to lighthouses and lightships. It is open every day from July to September. For winter opening hours, telephone 01326 290202.

CADGWITH AND THE SERPENTINE ROUTE

DISTANCE/TIME	4.5 miles (7.2km) / 3hrs
ASCENT/GRADIENT	230ft (70m) / ▲
PATHS	Very good, occasionally rocky in places; rocks may be slippery when wet
LANDSCAPE	Landlocked lanes and woodland tracks, coastal footpaths high above the sea
SUGGESTED MAP	AA Walker's Map 10 Land's End & The Lizard
START/FINISH	Grid reference: SW720146
DOG FRIENDLINESS	May be off lead on coastal paths, but keep under strict control on field paths
PARKING	Cadgwith car park, about 350yds (320m) from Cadgwith (busy in summer)
PUBLIC TOILETS	Ruan Minor and Cadgwith

The rock of the Lizard Peninsula is fascinating by name and by nature. Its geological label, serpentinite, is a word that fails to slither quite so easily off the tongue as does its popular usage, 'serpentine'. The name derives from the sinuous veins of green, red, yellow and white that wriggle across the dark green or brownish-red surface of the rock. The best-quality serpentine is easily carved and shaped, and can be polished to a beautiful sheen. You can admire the rock on this route, where the stiles are built of serpentine slabs – their surfaces are mirror-smooth and slippery from use (take care when wet).

In the 19th century, serpentine furnishings were the height of fashion and the material was used for shopfronts and fireplaces. The industry declined during the 1890s, due partly to the vagaries of fashion but also because the colourful, curdled stone of the Lizard decayed quickly in polluted urban atmospheres. Cheaper, more resilient marble from Italy and Spain began to dominate the market. Today serpentine craftsmen still operate in workshops on the Lizard, and you can buy serpentine souvenirs at Lizard village. At Carleon Cove, halfway through the walk, you'll find the ruins of waterwheels, steam engines, machine shops, storehouses and a factory where serpentine was processed until the early 1890s. Today Carleon Cove is in the care of the National Trust.

From Carleon Cove the coast path is followed to Cadgwith, an archetypal Cornish fishing village. Cadgwith has a number of thatched cottages, a rare sight in windy Cornwall. The village still supports a fleet of fishing boats, launched from the shingle beach, and is given an enduring identity because of it. Cadgwith's profile rose even higher after the BBC TV series *The Fisherman's Apprentice* (2012), featuring the marine biologist Monty Halls learning the hard skills of small-boat fishing, was filmed here. Beyond the village the coast path leads to the Devil's Frying Pan, a vast gulf in the cliffs caused by the collapse of a section of coast that had been undermined by the sea.

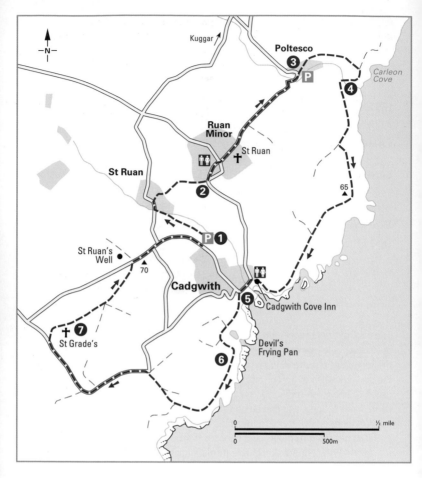

1. Leave the car park by the far end following the 'Footpath to Village' sign. Immediately after turn left along a grassy ride just below the car park, and follow this along to a stile. Bear right off the track to continue through a gate and then on into woodland. Turn right at a lane, and cross a stream, then on the corner, go up a track and continue along to the main road at Ruan Minor.

2. Go left and, just beyond the shop, turn left down a surfaced path. Rejoin the main road by a thatched cottage (there are toilets just before the road). Cross diagonally right, then go down a lane next to a school and pass the Church of St Ruan.

3. In 0.3 miles (500m), just past an old mill and a bridge, go right at a T-junction to reach the car park at Poltesco. Here you may drop into the National Trust's free exhibition in a converted barn about the local area and the serpentine factory. From the far end of the car park go through a gate and follow a track. Go right at a junction. Look out for a bench covered in bas relief pilchards.

4. Go over a wooden bridge above the cove, then turn left at a T-junction and again turn left in 0.25 miles (400m) where the path branches. Go through a kissing gate and continue along the cliff-edge path (with care in places) to Cadgwith. At the road, turn left and pass through the commercial hub of the village.

5. Follow a narrow path next to a house called 'Long Loft'. By a house gateway, go left up a surfaced path, signposted 'Devil's Frying Pan'. At an open area turn left, pass Townplace Cottage, cross a meadow and reach the Devil's Frying Pan itself. Continue along the coast path for about 0.4 miles (0.6km).

6. At a junction, by a little runnel and stile, follow a path inland and uphill to a T-junction with a rough track. Turn left and then, at a public lane, go left again and after 0.5 miles (800m) turn through a wooden field gate signed 'St Grada's Church' and along a track to St Grade's (or St Grada's) church. Follow a short path along the outside of the church wall to reach a wooden stile.

7. Follow the left-hand field-edge behind the church to the left corner, then go over a stone stile. Go straight across the field and then cross a wooden stile onto a road. St Ruan's Well is opposite diagonally left. Turn right for 200yds (183m), then branch off right between stone pillars to return to the car park.

Where to eat and drink

The Cadgwith Cove Inn at Cadgwith has a good selection of pub food including seafood linguine and fresh mussels as well as a vegetarian dish of the day, home-made burgers and fish and chips to take away. The Old Cellars Restaurant in Cadgwith is licensed and features the courtyard of an old pilchard processing 'cellars' right opposite Cadgwith harbour beach. The restaurant serves morning coffee, lunch, afternoon tea with tasty home-made cakes, and evening meals.

What to see

Water is often slow to drain on the soil of the Cadgwith and Lizard areas due to the impermeable nature of the underlying rock. This results in the development of many marshy areas known as wet flushes, which support moisture-loving plants. There are several places where you should see the greater horsetail, an attractive, exotic-looking plant that has long feathery branches and segmented flower stalks. On the coast proper look for the sturdy tree mallow, a tall plant with hairy stem and purple flowers.

While you're there

The Church of St Ruan is a small, endearing building built mainly of local serpentine stone. It has a low tower, as if bitten off by the notorious Lizard wind. The east window is dedicated to Thomas Richard Collinson Harrison, a 16-year-old boy who died in a cliff fall in 1909.

COVERACK
TO COVENTRY

DISTANCE/TIME	2 miles (3.2km) / 1hr 30min
ASCENT/GRADIENT	390ft (119m) / ▲ ▲
PATHS	Woodland and coastal paths, roads
LANDSCAPE	A complex coastal area of rocky pinnacles and wooded hinterland
SUGGESTED MAP	AA Walker's Map 10 Land's End & The Lizard
START/FINISH	Grid reference: SW786182
DOG FRIENDLINESS	Off lead but under control near houses
PARKING	Small car park at Dolor Point, or a public car park at the entrance to Coverack, coming from Helston on the B3294
PUBLIC TOILETS	By main car park and before the Paris Hotel
NOTES	If parking at the main car park, you need to walk through Coverack to the start. There and back is an additional 0.5 miles (800m)

Coverack may seem well protected from Cornwall's westerly storms by its east-facing location and the protective bulwarks of Lizard Head and the nearby Black Head. This can be a stormy place, however, and an enduring reminder of this is the name of the village's famous Paris Hotel, named after a ship that was wrecked here in 1899. Coverack is still a favoured place, and is hugely popular with beach-loving families and with windsurfers.

The village's strong identity was forged in medieval times when Coverack was a thriving pilchard fishing port. Its modern name derives from the medieval name Porthcovrek, one meaning of which is 'the cove (*porth*) of the stream'. Fishing continued from Coverack throughout the centuries, but declined from the early 20th century onwards when pilchard numbers dwindled. This could have been because of overfishing, but also because of the mysterious behaviour of fish species that often seem to abandon waters without reason. Fishing boats still work from Coverack's tiny harbour, and it is just beyond the harbour where this walk begins at Dolor Point, the far seaward end of the village.

Head south from Dolor Point through Coverack's attractive cottages and public spaces, soon reaching the coast path and Chynhalls Point, a narrow rocky headland around which a circuit is made, including the rocky summit. An Iron Age promontory settlement is thought to have been sited here. Below is Porthbeer Cove, with its wide apron of flat, sea-stained rock and an outer area of sand that is covered at high tide. The steep slopes that rise above Porthbeer are fascinating. Beyond here the path moves inland and through woods to visit an extraordinary Terence Coventry sculpture garden. The final stroll back to Coverack is untaxing, and once again draws a sharp contrast between the rawness of the wild coastline and the picturesque village.

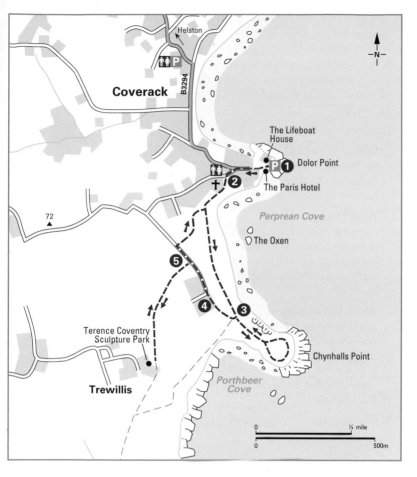

1. Join the coastal footpath at the inner corner of the car park and follow the path above a rocky beach. Pass behind a house and go right, up steep stone steps. Follow the path past several benches to reach the road.

2. Turn left. In a few paces leave the road, and go straight ahead along a surfaced path to the left of an old Wesleyan chapel. Pass in front of a row of cottages. At the first junction leave the surfaced path and take the left-hand path, signed 'Coast Path Kennack Sands'. Keep left at a junction by a stone bench.

3. At a junction of paths, turn sharp left to explore Chynhalls Point. Bear right at a fork to reach the summit before dropping down on a narrow and steep path the other side. Fork left just after the summit to follow a path that contours anti-clockwise around the headland, passing a row of rusting fence posts and returning to the junction at waypoint 3. Carry straight on up the hill. At a junction of paths, turn left up some steps.

4. At the top of the steps bear right on a lane to pass some cottages and shortly after turn left along a footpath signed 'Sculpture Park'. Cross a stream and keep right. The Terence Coventry Sculpture Park extends over ground on

both sides of the path, so have a good wander around both the upper and lower sections of this unusual attraction. Afterwards, retrace your steps to the road and turn left.

5. Turn right at a footpath by two sturdy granite gateposts. Follow this down as it dives beneath wind-sculpted hawthorns down steps and back to the signpost for Kennack Sands, as seen earlier. Continue forward to retrace your steps to the car park.

Where to eat and drink

For fish and chips as close to the sea as it gets, try the Lifeboat House. Across the way is the bar of the Paris Hotel, as famous for its folk music sessions as for its pub food.

What to see

Along the middle section of the walk south of Polbrean Cove is an area of wet flushes where tall reeds grow. Such habitats support plants like bog asphodel, which have bright yellow flowers. Another moisture-loving coastal plant is cotton grass, easily identified by its 'cotton bud' flower heads.

While you're there

The uniquely talented sculptor and farmer Terence Coventry lives and works near Coverack and has created a compelling sculpture park that can be visited from the route of this walk. A number of sculptures are displayed in meadows to either side of the path, and the experience of walking through them is inspiring. There is no charge, but you enter at your own risk.

PORTHOUSTOCK
TO ST KEVERNE

DISTANCE/TIME	4 miles (6.4km) / 2hrs 30 min
ASCENT/GRADIENT	606ft (185m) / ▲ ▲ ▲
PATHS	Field-edge paths, coastal footpath, steeply stepped path, country lanes, many stiles
LANDSCAPE	Fields, woods and coast
SUGGESTED MAP	AA Walker's Map 10 Land's End & The Lizard
START/FINISH	Grid reference: SW807218
DOG FRIENDLINESS	Dogs on lead through grazed areas and as notices indicate
PARKING	Large area of parking on grass and gravel above beach. Donation box
PUBLIC TOILETS	Porthoustock
NOTES	Porthoustock Quarry is a working quarry. Please heed all warning notices. Blasting may take place at any time

The heart has been torn out of the Cornish coast below the attractive village of St Keverne, at the great quarries of Porthoustock and Dean Point, but the contrast between this oddly compelling landscape and the green fields and woods around St Keverne makes for a fascinating walking experience. There has been an honourable trade in quarrying here for many years. Porthoustock Quarry lies on the south side of Porthoustock Cove and is a working quarry. Dean Quarry is currently mothballed, but there are plans to re-open it. Part of this walk follows the coastal footpath around Dean Quarries.

The sea along this section of the Cornish coast has a dramatic and often grim history. About a mile southeast of Porthoustock Cove lies the Manacles, a dangerous area of partially submerged rocks that lurk just under a mile (1.6km) offshore from Godrevy Beach. The Manacles rocks can be clearly seen at low tide from the part of the walk that descends to Godrevy Beach. Scores of vessels were wrecked on this notorious reef, especially during the days of sail. Many hundreds of lives were lost in harrowing circumstances – although there is a noble record of lifesaving by local people. The name Manacles is a corruption of the Cornish Maen Eglos, which translates rather menacingly as the 'Church Stone'. Today the area round the Manacles is one of the most popular diving spots in the country, and dive boats launch regularly from Porthoustock beach.

The maritime history of the St Keverne area included formidable smuggling activity until well into the 19th century. In 1762, at Porthoustock, 218 barrels of brandy were landed in one night. There were few qualms about sharing the spoils, and St Keverne's Three Tuns Inn is said to have been named after three kegs of smuggled brandy that were found by excise men in 1467, in the possession of the local vicar. Dramatic politics also played a part in the history of the area during the 1497 Cornish Rebellion against the raising of taxes by Henry VII to fund a war against Scotland. A St Keverne blacksmith, Michael Joseph, known as An Gof (the blacksmith), was a prominent leader of the rebellion. The rebel force reached as far as southeast London, where they were defeated by Henry's army. Michael An Gof, together with his co-leader Thomas Flamank, were hung, drawn and quartered as traitors, but are hailed to this day as true Cornish heroes. A handsome statue of An Gof and Flamank (see While you're there) was unveiled in St Keverne in 1997 on the 500th anniversary of the rebellion.

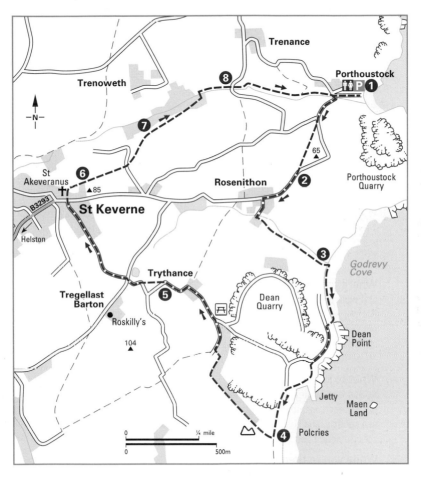

1. Turn left on leaving Porthoustock Beach car park and follow the road steeply uphill. Turn left at the first junction. In another steep 55yds (50m), go right and over a stile, then bear left across three fields to reach a lane.

2. Turn right and reach the little hamlet of Rosenithon, then turn left down a lane by a postbox. Where the lane ends at Chenhale, go left through a kissing gate. Follow a path through fields to reach Godrevy Beach. Dogs should be kept on leads until the beach.

3. Head for the south end of the beach and follow the coast path uphill to reach three large boulders and a quarry warning notice. Bear left down a broad track towards the sea and follow footpath notices round the edge of Dean Point and its quarries, passing above an old jetty and a small beach. Follow the path downhill to another warning sign and a junction with a path leading inland.

4. Go right, signed to St Keverne, and follow a very steep path uphill through woods. Continue through a kissing gate until you reach a broad gravel track by houses. Turn right along the track, passing a pleasant picnic area on the way, to where the track bends left and becomes a surfaced road.

5. In just under 0.5 miles (800m), at a sharp bend, look for a stile on the right. Use this stile to cut across a field and back on to the lane. At the next road junction you can divert left to Roskilly's Farm, famous for the delicious ice cream it produces. On the main route, keep ahead at the junction for just 0.5 miles (800m) to reach St Keverne and its landmark church.

6. Go into the churchyard and follow a footpath to the left of the church. Keep straight ahead at a junction with a wall on your right, go through a metal gate then go through a wooden kissing gate. Follow the obvious path along two fields. Cross a lane and then a stile, then keep to the left edge of a field.

7. Where the field-edge bends left, keep ahead following the contour of the field to reach a wooden stile and a gateway. Keep straight ahead on a path into woodland. Cross a small stream and a stile and then reach some stone steps at a junction. Turn right along a sunken lane.

8. At a road, turn left uphill, then in 50yds (46m), turn off right. Cross a stream and then go through a dainty metal gate. Follow a path beneath trees to reach a lane by thatched cottages, from where you descend to Porthoustock.

Where to eat and drink

The walk passes close to Roskilly's, the working dairy farm of Tregellast Barton, where the Roskilly family have established a famous ice-cream parlour and restaurant, and a shop selling mouthwatering fudge, jams, chutneys, apple juice and cider. There are two pubs in St Keverne, the Three Tuns Hotel and the White Hart, both of which do bar meals.

What to see

At Godrevy Beach a variety of salt-resistant plants cover the inner section of the beach, including sea plantain with its tall, greenish spikes, sea beet, sea splurge, and sea bindweed, with its white bell-like flowers. All are specially equipped to cope with the extremes of their environment,.

While you're there

While you're in St Keverne, visit the Church of St Akeveranus. It dates from the 15th century but the octagonal spire was renewed in the late 18th century after it was damaged by lightning. Before the introduction of modern navigation aids the spire was a crucial landmark that sailors relied on in clear weather to identify the infamous Manacles reef. Check out the statue to Cornish heroes Michael An Gof and Thomas Flamank located just outside the village centre on the B3293 Helston road.

A HELFORD
ESTUARY CIRCUIT

DISTANCE/TIME	5 miles (8km) / 3hrs
ASCENT/GRADIENT	328ft (100m) / ▲
PATHS	Good woodland paths and tracks and field paths. Short section of quiet lane, many stiles
LANDSCAPE	Wooded creekside and fields
SUGGESTED MAP	AA Walker's Map 10 Land's End & The Lizard
START/FINISH	Grid reference: SW759261
DOG FRIENDLINESS	Dogs must be kept under strict control between Treath and St Anthony and in all fields
PARKING	Helford car park overlooking the creek. Can become busy in summer. Only authorised cars are allowed beyond the car park into the village of Helford
PUBLIC TOILETS	Helford car park

The Helford River is enduringly popular with land-based visitors and leisure sailors alike, yet the area manages somehow to absorb it all. Cars probe tentatively between the unforgiving stone hedges of narrow Cornish lanes. The bulk of river craft are yachts, so that on a busy sailing day you will hear only the pleasing flap of sails blowing through. The trees that line the estuary and its subsidiary creeks play a great part in muffling the human racket.

The picturesque, leisure-dominated Helford of today was once a bustling haven for all sorts of trade, and was a haven for pirates and smugglers. During Elizabethan times especially, a posse of Cornish rascals, from the highest in the land to the lowest, were engaged in plundering the cargoes of vessels that sailed through the Channel approaches. The Helford, as it is popularly known, was a secretive, useful base from which all manner of goods could be spirited away inland. In later times the river became an equally secretive base for missions against German-occupied France during World War II. There is little physical evidence of any of this busy past, but in the shrouded creeks that run off like fibrous roots from the main river it is easy to imagine the utter remoteness of life hundreds of years ago, when movement by sea was far more convenient than by land.

This walk starts from the village of Helford and follows the southern shore of the estuary between Treath and Dennis Head, mainly through the deep woodland of the Bosahan estate. The return leg follows the north shore of the adjacent Gillan Creek, far smaller and thus far less accommodating to vessels than the deep Helford. Here the tiny Church of St Anthony adds to the overall serenity. From near the head of the creek, you climb inland to Manaccan, a charming village that seems to tumble down the slopes of the valley. Beyond the village the route leads into the wooded valley above Helford and takes you back to your starting point through chequered shade.

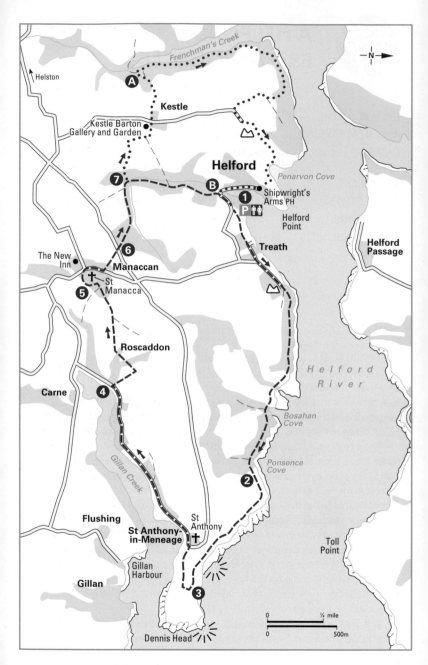

1. At the car park, opposite the entrance to the café, turn left along a path signposted 'Coast Path'. Go through a metal gate and then follow a sunken track. Descend some steps, then soon turn right along a lane. When you come to a steep right-hand bend, bear off ahead along a track. Follow this permissive path along through trees, passing some fine little beaches along the way.

2. Leave the wooded area via a kissing gate, then turn left along a field-edge to a stone stile. Follow the bottom edge of the next two fields. Go through a field gap beside a white pole and a post and triangle (navigation marks). Follow the field-edge ahead. Go through a kissing gate, then follow the field-edge (seat and viewpoint on the left). Go through a wooden kissing gate. Continue to the start of a wide track between gorse and low trees.

3. Turn sharply right at the start of the wide track and follow the left-hand field-edge, then go right along a waymarked path across the open field. Go through a gate to join a track behind a house and reach a road. Turn left and descend to St Anthony's Church. Follow the road alongside Gillan Creek.

4. Just past where the road curves round a bay, look carefully for a public footpath and go up right and through a gate. Follow a track through trees to houses at Roscaddon. Keep ahead along a track, then lane, to reach a T-junction with a road. Cross over and enter the churchyard of St Manacca.

5. Go through the churchyard and then the gate opposite to a road. Keep ahead to a junction (the New Inn is down to the left) then go up right, past the school. Keep uphill, then turn left along Minster Meadow, go along a path to the left of Kensa Kew, and through a field, used as a public car park, to a road.

6. Go diagonally left to the stile opposite, cross a field, then go left following the field-edge to reach a stile into the woods. Follow the path ahead. Go down three granite steps and in 10 yds (9m) reach a junction.

7. Follow the right-hand track (can be very muddy) to reach Helford by the bridge over the stream. Go up the road directly ahead to the car park.

Extending the walk At the junction at Point 7, keep straight on. Cross two small streams and go through trees to reach a stile. Cross the stile, turn right along field-edge to a gap then go sharp right along left edge of a field to a five-bar gate in the corner. Keep ahead between buildings, passing Kestle Barton Gallery. Cross a road, go over a grid and follow a track downhhill to Point A where a path goes right, signed 'Frenchman's Creek'. The path leads down the east bank of the creek then climbs steeply to a junction. Go left, signed 'Creekside Path'. At a T-junction with a metalled lane turn right. At the next T-junction (seat on left) turn right, signed 'Helford via Penarvon Cove'. On reaching a lane, turn immediately left down a lane signed 'Penghedwen and Helford (via Penarvon Cove)'. Fork right to reach Penarvon Cove. From the top end of the beach a path leads to a concrete track. A left turn leads past the Shipwright's Arms, through Helford village to join the main walk at Point B.

Where to eat and drink

Ice creams and drinks are available from the beach shop at St Anthony. Both South Café and The New Inn at Manaccan serve food, as does the Shipwright's Arms at Helford. By the car park, a converted church is home to the Holy Mackerel Café and Bar.

What to see

There are two interesting churches on the walk, one in St Anthony-in-Meneage and the other in Manaccan.

COAST AND RIVER AT MAWNAN SMITH

DISTANCE/TIME	4 miles (6.4km) / 2hr 30min
ASCENT/GRADIENT	242ft (74m) / ▲ ▲
PATHS	Good coastal and field paths, short sections of road walking; many stiles
LANDSCAPE	Wooded riverbank and low coastline
SUGGESTED MAP	AA Walker's Map 10 Land's End & The Lizard
START/FINISH	Grid reference: SW787272
DOG FRIENDLINESS	Lead required for field sections and roads
PARKING	By Mawnan Church (fee charged)
PUBLIC TOILETS	Opposite The Red Lion pub in Mawnan Smith (on road to Helford Passage)

The quiet waters and wooded banks of the Helford River inspire thoughts of tall sailing ships stealing through dawn mist. Sails are still in evidence today, and during spring and summer you'll see a constant to-ing and fro-ing of yachts across the mouth of the river as they tack into the sanctuary of the Helford and head upriver. The Helford is where the famous Cornish novelists Arthur Quiller-Couch and Daphne du Maurier set their romantic stories.

The Helford's cross-Channel connections are historic. French privateers and smugglers were united with their Cornish brethren through smuggling – a respected, though illegal, business during the 18th and 19th centuries. Seagoers, legitimate and otherwise, would have used the river as a perfect hiding place from storms and the authorities. The Helford was later used during World War II by the Special Operations Executive (SOE), which sent specially adapted boats, disguised as Breton fishing vessels, to mingle with the French fishing fleet. These vessels and their crews passed on special agents, equipment and information under the eyes of a German-crewed overseer vessel. Today the French connection is a strong as ever, with countless sailing trips to Brittany starting from the river.

Mawnan Church stands on the site of a prehistoric earthwork. An original structure was erected in the 13th century, but changes have taken place over the years. In spite of clumsy restoration work of the early 19th century, the building retains great character. The name Mawnan again underlines the area's strong connections with France, as it is believed to have been the name of a Breton monk who settled here during the 6th century AD. The site is possibly Bronze Age and Iron Age, a typical progression in the siting of Cornish religious buildings. There are 13th-century remnants, not least a fine piscina – a water basin with carved heads – in the wall of the chancel. You can try out your Cornish language, Kernewek, at the 19th-century lychgate, whose inscription translates as 'It is good for me to draw nigh unto God'.

The first part of the walk makes its pleasant way from Mawnan Church via a lane and then a field path to the coast, and then follows the coast path round Toll Point, overlooking the mouth of the Helford River. As the route leads away from the coast and along the north shore of the river the value of Helford as a sheltered anchorage becomes obvious. The mix of wild foreshore with a hinterland of lush green fields and woods is a token of long-term ownership by grand estates, which created an almost park-like ambience that sits happily with the natural beauty of the river. The National Trust now owns a good section of the riverbank south of Mawnan Smith, and maintains this sense of beauty and serenity for all. From a little stony beach at Porth Saxon, the route heads inland to the outskirts of the village of Mawnan Smith and then leads back to the coast at Rosemullion Head and so back to Mawnan Church, where a visit to the churchyard uncovers history in stone.

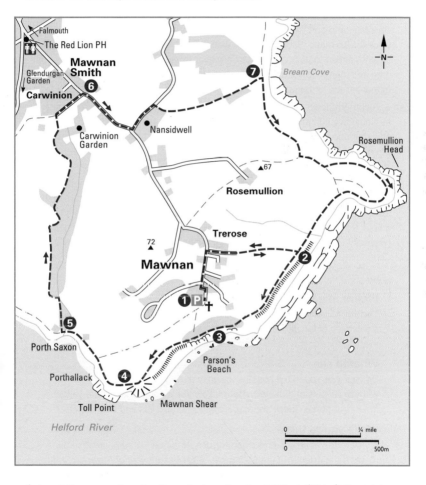

1. Leave the car park and walk up the lane for about 300yds (274m). Turn right through a gate, between the entrances to houses, and follow a public footpath along a track. Go over a stile and follow the left-hand edge of a field.

2. Join the coast path at the seaward corner of the field. Turn right and follow the coast path along the edge of the field, to go through a wooden kissing gate.

3. Continue along the coast path for just over 0.5 miles (800m). Emerge from the woods and go through a kissing gate into a field. Keep straight ahead along the field-edge, with views of the Helford River.

4. Go through a kissing gate by a wooden bench, and over a stone stile. Follow the path, soon descending some steps, and continue along the river's edge. Go through a wooden kissing gate into a field and keep straight ahead, descending steeply. Go through a kissing gate and cross above the small stony beach at Porthallack. Ignore the footpath going inland. Turn right to the left of a boathouse, go through a kissing gate and turn left along the field edge. Go over a stile, pass another boathouse and cross above Porth Saxon beach.

5. Pass in front of yet another boathouse, and then turn sharply right off the coast path by a National Trust sign for 'Carwinion' and follow a track inland. Go into a field and, in 30yds (33m), go through a gate and follow a wide stony track for 0.5 miles (800m) through woodland. Cross a slate bridge and continue straight ahead to pass alongside Carwinion garden. Climb steeply to a wooden gate and then follow a track. At a junction by Carwinion Cottage keep right and follow a track to the public road on the outskirts of Mawnan Smith.

6. Turn right down the road, walking with care. Keep round left at a junction by Nansidwell. In just over 300yds (300m) turn right, go over a concrete stile and continue down a driveway. Go through a gate and follow a path down to the coast.

7. In sight of a small, rocky beach, turn right and follow the narrow coast path. At Rosemullion Head, bear off left along a barely discernible path, and skirt round the seaward edge of the Head. Join the coast path, which becomes the lower, less prominent of the two paths. Cross a wooden bridge and a stile into a field. Go over another stone stile into a field and turn immediately right (waypoint 2 of the walk). Go steeply up the field edge to reach a stile by a gate. Continue to the road and turn left to reach Mawnan Church and the car park.

Where to eat and drink
The attractive Red Lion pub in the square at Mawnan Smith village offers a selection of lunch dishes as well as ciabattas and soup. It also does evening meals, and has a good selection of beers and other drinks.

What to see
On your way round the coast, especially during spring and summer, you will see carpets of bluebells that make a fine display against the yellow flowers of gorse. There are also early purple orchids and wild violets.

While you're there
A visit to the nearby Glendurgan Garden (National Trust) is an absolute must. The garden is about 0.25 miles (400m) southwest of Mawnan Smith on the road to the village of Durgan. This lovely garden, in its almost sub-tropical valley, was established in the 1820s and 1830s by the Quaker industrialist Alfred Fox. The garden contains a wealth of trees and exotic plants including New Zealand tree ferns, while familiar species include azaleas, hydrangeas and camellias. There is an entertaining maze.

WALKING AROUND FALMOUTH

DISTANCE/TIME	3 miles (4.8km) / 3hrs
ASCENT/GRADIENT	197ft (60m) / ▲
PATHS	Surfaced walkways and paths. Very steep steps descend at end of walk
LANDSCAPE	Townscape and seafront
SUGGESTED MAP	AA Walker's Map 10 Land's End & The Lizard
START/FINISH	Grid reference: SW805327
DOG FRIENDLINESS	Dog fouling of streets is prohibited
PARKING	Quarry Car Park, Quarry Hill or the Moor Hornworks Car Park, Pendennis Castle
PUBLIC TOILETS	Webber Street; Prince of Wales Pier; North Quay Arwenack Street; Princess Pavilion

Modern Falmouth stands on the wide estuary of Carrick Roads, one of the world's largest natural harbours. It developed as a port after Henry VIII built a formidable castle on Pendennis Point, at the eastern part of the town, and another castle on the opposite headland at St Mawes. Pendennis Castle survives as one of the finest examples of Tudor fortifications in Britain. In the late 17th century Falmouth became a postal packet station from where fast brigantines carried mail, first to Spain and then as far as the Americas. Other developments included fishing, and shipbuilding and ship repairing. Today the town has a thriving tourist industry and is a leading educational centre hosting the Combined Universities of Cornwall as well as Falmouth Art College, a Marine School and a School of Mines.

The walk begins at The Moor, once a tidal creek and now a rather traffic-bound focal point of the town's busy commercial life. A short step takes you to Prince of Wales Pier, ever busy with river ferries. The walk then leads along Falmouth's main street, which is made up of the linked thoroughfares of Market Street, Church Street and Arwenack Street. The waterfront opens up now and the National Maritime Museum is passed on your left (see While you're there). The second part of the walk leads past Falmouth Docks and then heads along the bayside road of Cliff Walk to reach a little complex of Victorian grottoes and follies. These include the Gyllyngdune Gardens, created in the 1830s as part of the Gyllyngdune estate. Above the gardens is the Princess Pavilion, opened in 1911 and used still for public entertainment. Beyond here a pleasant stroll leads along the tree-lined central parade of Arwenack Avenue and on past Falmouth's Old Synagogue, which was built in 1808 and served the town's Jewish community until 1879. A little further on you reach the Jacob's Ladder Inn. Opposite is the start of 'Jacob's Ladder', whose 111 steep steps take you back to The Moor. It was built by a 19th-century merchant, Jacob Hamblyn, as a link between his house above and his workshop below.

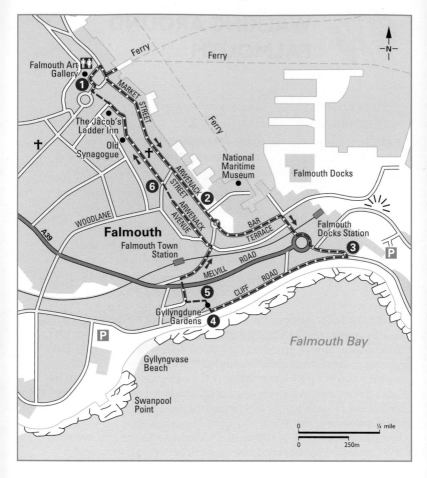

1. Walk down Webber Street past the Falmouth Art Gallery and to the left of the town hall. Cross the street diagonally right and visit the Prince of Wales Pier, from where you can enjoy estuary and waterfront views. Returning from the pier, turn left along Falmouth's busy main street, passing the entrances to other quays (see What to see) on the way and eventually reaching the National Maritime Museum.

2. Continue past a rather bleak-looking granite obelisk dating from the late 18th century. Go along Grove Place and bear round left along Marine Crescent, which becomes Bar Terrace. Cross over at a junction then, opposite the entrance to Falmouth Docks, bear right and go under a railway bridge. Cross with care at a roundabout, then continue up Castle Hill opposite. Keep right at the top of the rise at a junction with Pendennis Rise and continue along Castle Drive.

3. Turn right and follow Cliff Road alongside the sea for about 0.5 miles (0.8km). (To visit Pendennis Castle, keep straight ahead along Castle Drive from the junction with Cliff Road. Then retrace your steps to follow the walk route along Cliff Road.)

4. Pass a tiny building with a stairwell that leads down to a viewpoint. Just before a little Gothic folly cross the road with care. Go up the left-hand walkway of Gyllyngdune Gardens. In a few paces, go right down some steps and pass through a little sunken grotto, then continue up the steps opposite. (You can also reach this grotto by going through a narrow tunnel at road level, if its gate is unlocked.) Follow the walkway past two shell grottoes and continue ahead to reach a gate into the grounds of the Princess Pavilion.

5. Leave by the opposite left-hand corner of the Pavilion grounds and then through the Pavilion's entranceway. Go down the steps between the brick pillars and then go right down Gyllyngvase Terrace to a junction with Melvill Road. Cross the road diagonally right and go down some steps, then turn right along Avenue Road. Follow the road downhill and go beneath a railway bridge, then turn left along the peaceful, tree-lined central parade of Arwenack Avenue.

6. Walk between the flanking pillars at the end of the avenue, cross Swanpool Street, with care, and keep ahead along Gyllyng Street to its end. Keep up to the left where the street forks, pass the brick-fronted Old Synagogue and keep left at a fork to go along Vernon Place. Bear round to the left by The Jacob's Ladder Inn, then, just opposite the pub, turn right, brace yourself, and descend the steps of Jacob's Ladder, carefully, to The Moor.

Where to eat and drink

Falmouth has an extensive range of cafés and restaurants, and on the route of the walk you'll pass various traditional inns such as the Grapes Inn and The Jacob's Ladder Inn. There is a licensed café and restaurant at the Princess Pavilion and a tea room at Pendennis Castle. The castle has a range of picnic spots and there are also lots of seats for picnics along Cliff Road and on the beach walkways down below.

What to see

You can divert from Falmouth's busy, shop-lined main street to visit the waterfront quays of Fish Strand Quay, by the Grapes Inn and Upton Slip in Church Street, where you'll find the colourful figurehead of an old ship, the *Amazon*. On Custom House Quay there is a tall, red-brick chimney stack, called the King's Pipe, and this was once used to burn off the smuggled tobacco that had been confiscated by excisemen.

While you're there

Visit Falmouth's award-winning Art Gallery (open 10–5, Monday–Saturday) and the outstanding National Maritime Museum (open 10–5, every day; closed Christmas day and Boxing Day) on Discovery Quay off Arwenack Street. You can also add a visit to Pendennis Castle (see waypoint 3). Check www.english-heritage.org.uk for details of the seasonal opening times for Pendennis Castle.

BY THE FAL ESTUARY

DISTANCE/TIME	4 miles (6.4km) / 3hrs
ASCENT/GRADIENT	164ft (50m) / ▲
PATHS	Good paths throughout. Wooded section to Trelew Farm is often very wet, several stiles
LANDSCAPE	Wooded peninsula flanked by river estuaries and creeks
SUGGESTED MAP	AA Walker's Map 10 Land's End & The Lizard
START/FINISH	Grid reference: SW820352
DOG FRIENDLINESS	Dogs on lead through grazed areas and churchyard
PARKING	Mylor Churchtown car park
PUBLIC TOILETS	Mylor Churchtown and Flushing

The inner estuary of the River Fal, the Carrick Roads, is reputedly the third largest natural harbour in the world. It has welcomed all manner of vessels, from Tudor warships to fishing fleets, to modern cargo vessels and oil rigs and a growing number of yachts. Part of the maritime heritage of the Fal belongs to the Post Office Packet Service that was responsible for communications throughout the British Empire. This was based in the Fal from 1689 to 1850, a glorious and lawless period of British seafaring. Fast Packet vessels ran south to Spain and Portugal and then on to the Americas. The Packet sailors were notorious for their opportunism, and many a Packet ship returned with more than half its cargo as contraband goods. The main Packet base was at Falmouth, but Mylor was a servicing and supplies yard for the Packet boats and many of the captains lived at Flushing.

At Mylor today, maritime traditions are as strong as ever, as far as leisure sailing goes. Boatyards still bustle with work and there is a thriving sailing club. Such clubs are noted for producing accomplished sailors, and the Olympic gold medallist Ben Ainslie learnt many of his skills in these waters. Today, every creek and inlet of the Fal is dense with leisure craft. Modern Flushing is a peaceful backwater, within shouting distance of bustling Falmouth, but with the river between.

The walk takes you from Mylor along the shores of the blunt headland between Mylor Creek and the Penryn River and on to Flushing, in full view of Falmouth docks. Flushing is a charming enclave of handsome houses, many with Dutch features. From Flushing you turn inland and on to a delightful old track. This runs down a wooded valley to the tree-shrouded waters of Mylor Creek from where quiet lanes lead back to St Mylor Church. Here, in a churchyard that resonates with maritime history, stands the Ganges Memorial erected in 1872, a commemoration of 53 youngsters who died, mainly of disease, on the famous Royal Naval training ship HMS *Ganges*, which was based at Mylor from 1866 to 1899.

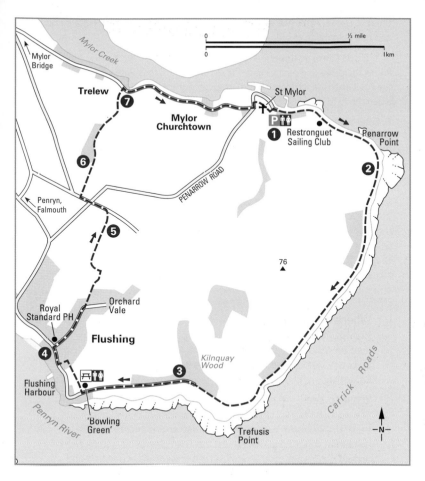

1. From the car park entrance, turn right to reach the start of a surfaced lane, signposted to Flushing. Follow the lane, then, by the gateway of a house, bear left along a path. Pass in front of Restronguet Sailing Club and keep to the right of a detached building.

2. Follow the path round Penarrow Point and continue round Trefusis Point. Reach a gate and granite grid stile by a wooden shack at Kilnquay Wood. Continue along a track, which shortly becomes surfaced.

3. Continue along the public road for 0.5 miles (0.8km). Where the road drops down towards the water's edge, bear right up a surfaced slope to the grassy area of the 'Bowling Green'. (Strictly no dog fouling, please.) Continue past a little pavilion and toilets and go down a surfaced path. Just beyond two seats, turn sharply left down a narrow path. Go down some steps and continue down a lane. At a street junction (Flushing's attractive little harbour is just to the left) turn right and go along the main street of the village.

4. At a junction by the Royal Standard, keep right and go up Kersey Road. At the top of the road, by Orchard Vale, go left up steps, signposted 'Mylor

Church'. Cross a stile and keep to the left field-edge to reach an isolated house and to a stile made of granite bollards.

5. In 25yds (23m) go through a gateway then turn left over a cattle grid and follow the drive to a public road, Penarrow Road. Cross with care, and go down the road opposite for 30yds (27m), then go right down steps, by a gate, and on down the field-edge.

6. Enter woodland and keep right at a junction to follow a rocky path that is often a mini-stream after heavy rainfall. Go through a gate, and walk onwards Go through the remains of a tiny gate, keep ahead, cross a stream and join a farm track. Turn right to reach a surfaced road at Trelew.

7. Turn right along the lane, passing an old water pump. When you get to a slipway, keep ahead along the unsurfaced track. Continue along between granite posts and on to join the public road into Mylor Churchtown. Cross the road with care (this is a blind corner) and go through the churchyard of St Mylor (please note the path through the churchyard is not a public right of way). Turn right when you reach the waterfront to find the car park in Mylor Churchtown.

Where to eat and drink
Halfway through the route, at Flushing, there are two good pubs, the Seven Stars and the Royal Standard. At Mylor Bridge, you'll find Castaways Wine Bar and Castaways east pub next door, as well as Café Mylor.

What to see
The wooded sections of the walk are composed mainly of deciduous trees. Unlike conifer woods, these diverse environments support numerous flowering plants amidst their damp, tangled, humus-rich undergrowth. Look for the pink and red flowers of herb Robert and campion, and the starry white blooms of greater stitchwort. This latter plant was believed to have curative properties in earlier times; it was ground into a paste and applied to boils and sores.

While you're there
Visit the parish church of St Mylor and the HMS *Ganges* memorial in the churchyard. The church has a gnomic tower and a campanile (a separate tower) houses the church bells. The *Ganges* was a famous Victorian training ship that moved to Harwich in 1899 and became a shore establishment in 1905. The original *Ganges* was a three-masted sailing gunship, built in Bombay and the last of its kind to sail round Cape Horn.

ROSELAND PENINSULA AND ST ANTHONY HEAD

DISTANCE/TIME	5.6 miles (9km) / 3hrs 30min
ASCENT/GRADIENT	230ft (70m) / ▲ ▲
PATHS	Excellent coastal and creekside footpaths. May be muddy in places during wet weather, many stiles
LANDSCAPE	Picturesque headland with open coast on one side and sheltered tidal creek and estuary on the other
SUGGESTED MAP	OS Explorer 105 Falmouth & Mevagissey
START/FINISH	Grid reference: SW848313
DOG FRIENDLINESS	Dogs on lead through grazed areas
PARKING	National Trust St Anthony Head car park. Can be busy in summer. Alternative parking at Porth Farm (waypoint 3, SW 868329)
PUBLIC TOILETS	St Anthony Head car park and Porth Farm car park

St Anthony Head lies at the tip of the most southerly promontory of the beautiful Roseland Peninsula, and was always of strategic importance. There was a gun battery on St Anthony Head from the early 19th century until 1957, its purpose being to defend the key port of Falmouth. The lighthouse on the Head was built in 1834. One of its main purposes is to warn vessels of the highly dangerous reefs known as the Manacles that lie offshore from Porthoustock below St Keverne.

As early as 1805, guns were positioned on St Anthony Head to cover the approaches to Falmouth. By the end of the 19th century the headland had been transformed into a formidable gun battery that remained either active or in readiness until after World War II. By 1957 Coastal Artillery was discontinued and the St Anthony Battery was stripped of its ordnance. The site came into the care of the National Trust in 1959.

The route of this walk starts from above the lighthouse and makes a circuit of the narrow peninsula behind St Anthony Head. The first part of the walk lies along the breezy east side of the peninsula. The path soon passes above the cliff-fringed Porthbeor Beach. Another half-mile takes you to the splendid Towan Beach within its sheltering bay. From Porth, above the beach, the route heads inland and follows the opposite side of the peninsula. Leafy paths wind along the peaceful wooded shores of Porth Creek and the Percuil River to pass the 19th-century Place House and St Anthony's Church. Beyond the church a more open coast is reached. The path now takes you south along the sea's edge back to St Anthony Head, where you can visit the lighthouse at certain times and also take a detour to see the old Observation Post on the high ground above (see While you're there).

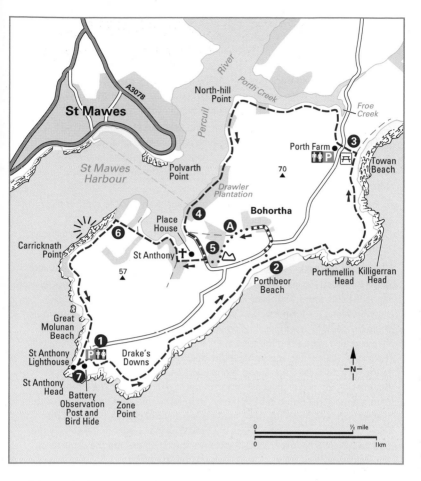

1. Leave the St Anthony Head car park at its far end and keep straight ahead along a surfaced lane past a row of holiday cottages on the left. Follow the coast path, running parallel with the old military road alongside Drake's Downs, to where it passes above Porthbeor Beach at a junction with what was the beach access path until a rock-fall closed it, as indicated by a sign.

2. Follow the coast path round Porthmellin Head and Killigerran Head to reach Towan Beach. At the junction with the beach access path, turn left and inland. Bear off left before a gate and go through a roofed passage to reach a road.

3. Go straight across the road and through a gapway, signed 'Porth Farm', then go down a surfaced drive. Turn into the entrance to the National Trust car park, then bear off left along a path signed 'Riverside Footpath Place Quay'. Go down a drive and soon turn right along a waymarked path. Cross a footbridge and turn right. Follow Froe Creek then follow a path alongside Porth Creek, through fields and woods and through Drawler Plantation, ignoring side paths.

4. Pass a small jetty where the St Mawes ferry picks up passengers. Continue to a gate on your right and onto the road end in front of Place House. Go left along the road and then head uphill for 160yds (150m).

5. Turn right and cross a stile, signposted 'Church of St Anthony and St Anthony Head'. Follow the path past the graves to the church. Keep dogs under control here. Go up the steps opposite the church door and follow a shady path uphill. Keep right at a junction signed 'St Anthony Head' and then at the next junction with a broad track turn left. At the beginning of the driveway to Cellars Cottage, go left through a gate into a field. Follow the edge of the field uphill then go through a kissing gate and head downhill to the water's edge.

6. Turn left and follow the coast path around Carricknath Point. Just past Great Molunan Beach, cross a causewayed dam above a small quay, then, at a junction, keep right and follow the coast path signs. At a junction with a surfaced track coming down from the left, keep straight ahead to St Anthony Lighthouse.

7. Return to the junction and climb the steep, surfaced track to reach the car park. Halfway up, another track leads off right to the preserved Battery Observation Post and to the bird hide above Zone Point. Just past this turn, at another junction, keep right and go up steps to reach the car park.

Shortening the walk This shorter walk concentrates on the most westerly end of the Roseland Peninsula around St Anthony Head. Follow the main walk as far as the cliff above Porthbeor Beach. Here, turn inland, following a blank signpost along the former access path to the beach, waypoint 2 on the main route to reach the road that runs down the spine of the peninsula. Cross the stile and turn right along the road, then, in just a few paces go left, signposted 'Bohortha'. Follow the lane through the quiet hamlet and where the road bends to the right, take the track ahead, signposted 'Place Quay 1/3m'. This track becomes a path and ends at a junction of paths, Point A. Take the left-hand path, signposted 'Church of St Anthony', then follow the field-edge downhill to reach a narrow stile on the right, and a steep flight of descending steps that takes you to a surfaced lane. Cross the road diagonally right to the stile by the gate (waypoint 5 on main route). From here the directions are the same as on the main walk.

Where to eat and drink
In summer there is often an ice cream and soft drinks van located at St Anthony Head car park. There's also a tea van run by the Thirstea Company by the National Trust archway at Porth. They serve pasties, rolls, cakes and tea from 11am to 5pm between Easter and October.

What to see
In the sheltered waters of Porth Creek and the Percuil River, look out for the heron and other wading birds such as curlews and oystercatchers. Around St Anthony Head, the various viewpoints offer opportunities for spotting seabirds such as the fulmar, cormorant, kittiwake and gannet.

While you're there
St Anthony Lighthouse is open to visitors at certain times, depending on lighthouse duties. Halfway up the path between lighthouse and car park, you can divert to the right along a path that takes you to a bird hide.

AROUND NARE HEAD

DISTANCE/TIME	7 miles (11.3km) / 5hrs
ASCENT/GRADIENT	1,312ft (400m) / ▲ ▲ ▲
PATHS	Good coastal footpath, field paths and quiet lanes. Field stiles are often overgrown, many stiles
LANDSCAPE	Vegetated coast with some cliffs. Mainly flat fields on inland section
SUGGESTED MAP	OS Explorer 105 Falmouth & Mevagissey
START/FINISH	Grid reference: SW906384
DOG FRIENDLINESS	Dogs on lead through grazed areas
PARKING	Carne Beach car park. Large National Trust car park behind beach
PUBLIC TOILETS	Carne Beach; Portloe; Veryan

There are parts of the Cornish coast that seem especially remote, where human development has not gone beyond farming and small-scale sea-going. The lonely stretch of south Cornish coast between Gerrans Bay and Veryan Bay, with Nare Head at its centre, is one such place.

The walk begins at the seasonally popular Carne Beach. A steady hike along the coast path from here soon brings you to a steep descent into the narrow Paradoe, pronounced 'Perada', Cove. On a spur of land above the sea is the ruin of a small cottage. This was the home of a 19th-century fisherman called Mallet, who lived during the week in this lonely spot, fishing from 'Mallet's Cove' below, then returning at weekends to his wife at the village of Veryan, just a few miles inland. Eventually Mallet emigrated to Australia – without his wife. The little ruined cottage above the restless sea still speaks of a life of extraordinary detachment.

From Paradoe it is a punishing climb to the flat top of Nare Head. Beyond the Head a pleasant ramble takes you along the coast past the steep Rosen Cliff and by lonely coves. Offshore lies the formidable Gull Rock, a busy seabird colony. The route leads to Portloe, a fishing village that seems to have survived without too much intrusion. Here, a steep-sided valley has left only enough room at its seaward end for fishing boats and a pleasant veneer of houses and cottages to either side. Head inland into a lost world of little fields and meadows that straggle across country to Veryan (see While you're there). From Veryan the route wanders back towards the sea, past the ancient landmark of Carne Beacon, a Bronze Age burial site that saw later service as a signal station, a triangulation point and a World War II observation post. A few fields away lies Veryan Castle, known also as the Ringarounds, the site of a late Iron Age farming settlement. These ancient sites prove that this absorbing landscape has given refuge to people for thousands of years. From the high ground the route leads down to the coast once more.

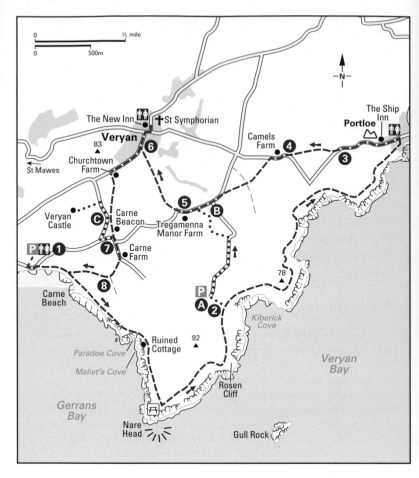

1. Turn left out of the car park and walk up the road, with care. Just past the steep bend, turn off right and go up some steps and on to the coast path. Keep right where a path leads off uphill to the left, and follow the coast path to Paradoe Cove and then continue past scenic Nare Head.

2. Above Kiberick Cove, go through a gap in a wall. Keep ahead through a dip to reach a kissing gate. After a National Trust sign for 'Broom Parc' bear right at a junction. Keep right at two further junctions and descend into Portloe. Go left up the road from the cove, past The Ship Inn.

3. Just after a sharp left-hand bend, and where the road narrows, go over a high step stile on the right. Cross a field to a stile, then follow the right field-edge. Pass a gate, then, in a few paces, go right and over a stile. Bear half left across the next field, heading for a white house, to reach a stile into a lane.

4. Go right along the road for 200yds (183m) past Camels Farm, then go left over a stile and immediately through a gate. Follow the right field-edge to another stile. Follow the next field-edge, then just before the field corner, go right over a stile. Turn left through a gap, then go diagonally half right across the next field to an overgrown stile. Head across the next field, aiming for the further right of a pair of telegraph poles, and exit onto a road via a stile so overgrown and neglected it is barely discernible. Turn left to a road junction. Continue along the road, signposted 'Carne and Pendower'.

5. Just past Tregamenna Manor Farm, on a bend, go over a stile by a gate on the right. Cut across the corner of the field, then go right over a stile. Cross the next field to a gate and then continue past a house on the left to a T-junction with a lane. (Turn right to visit Veryan.)

6. If you're not visiting Veryan village, turn left, then, just past Churchtown Farm, go left again over a stile. Turn left and follow the edge of the field to a stile into a lane. Go immediately left over a stile, then follow a path, past Carne Beacon, to a lane. If you're not visiting Veryan Castle, head straight on.

7. At a corner junction keep ahead down the lane, signposted 'Carne Village Only'. Bear right down a driveway past Beacon Cottage. Go downhill between houses. Follow the track round to the right between a garage and house, then follow a grassy track, keeping ahead at a junction.

8. Go through a gate (put dogs on leads here, please), and bear away right and then steeply downhill on a faint path to join the coast path back to Carne Beach and the car park at the start of the walk.

Shortening the walk The key to this shortened version of the walk is a path, established by the National Trust, that leads from the coast at waypoint 2 to a National Trust car park. Step through the gap in the wall, then turn sharply left and follow a path uphill and round to the right to reach a kissing gate into a lane end at Point A. Turn right and follow the lane inland to reach a right-hand bend just past a house. Go left and over a slate stile, follow the left edge of a field, then over another stile on the left. Bear half right to cross the next field to reach a stile, then bear half right towards a telegraph pole and go through a kissing gate along a fenced path to a stile by a road at Point B. Turn left here and follow the main walk route to waypoint 5 and onward. The area to the south of Veryan contains Veryan Castle, site of an Iron Age settlement. You can visit it by diverting from the route of this walk at Point C. Turn right along the lane and then first right to reach the access path to Veryan Castle on the left. Retrace your steps back to Point C and then continue along the route of the main walk to return to Carne Beach car park at the start of the walk.

Where to eat and drink
An ice cream van operates at Carne Beach in summer. Portloe's Ship Inn has a large beer garden and pub food. At Veryan, The New Inn has traditional food and fresh fish dishes. The Elerkey Guest House offers delicious Cornish cream teas.

What to see
Gull Rock, a short distance offshore from Nare Head, is a seabird colony that has belonged to the National Trust since 1989.

While you're there
Visit Veryan, one of south Cornwall's most fascinating villages, famous for its five whitewashed round houses with thatched conical roofs.

AROUND DODMAN POINT

DISTANCE/TIME	4.5 miles (7.2km) / 3hrs
ASCENT/GRADIENT	377ft (115m) / ▲ ▲
PATHS	Good coastal paths. Inland paths can be muddy, several stiles
LANDSCAPE	Open fields and coastal cliffs
SUGGESTED MAP	OS Explorer 105 Falmouth & Mevagissey
START/FINISH	Grid reference: SX011415
DOG FRIENDLINESS	Dogs on lead through grazed areas. Ponies graze the cliff-tops
PARKING	Gorran Haven car park, pay at kiosk
PUBLIC TOILETS	Gorran Haven

The high and lonely headland of Dodman Point thrusts its great bulk into the sea near Mevagissey and Gorran Haven, forming the eastern arch of Veryan Bay, on the south coast of Cornwall. To local people this dark and brooding promontory has always been the 'Deadman'. The source of the name may be prosaic, of course, a probable distortion of an ancient Cornish word; but 'Deadman' strikes a menacing echo with the nearby Vault Beach and such tideline rocks as the Bell and Mean-lay Rock that lie at the base of the 328ft (100m) Dodman cliffs. By whatever name, the Dodman is a natural fortress, and across its broad shoulders lies a massive earthen embankment, the landward defences of a promontory fort that dates back to the Iron Age.

The first part of the walk leads from the village of Gorran Haven along the coastal footpath to the great sweep of Vault Beach, or Bow Beach as it is also known. From above the beach the path rises steadily to the broad-backed promontory of the Dodman. The headland is crowned with a granite cross placed there in 1896 by the Reverend George Martin, rector of nearby St Michael Caerhays. Whether the cross was placed as a navigation aid or as a religious gesture is not clear. The inscription on the cross argues for Martin's religious certainties above all. Just inland from the cross (see waypoint 4), but hidden by scrub, is the Dodman Watch House, a survivor of the late 18th century. This much-restored little building was an Admiralty signal station, part of a chain of similar structures along the English Channel Coast. It was used in later years by coastguards and was restored by the National Trust.

From the Dodman, the route follows the coast path for a short distance along the headland's western flank to where a gate allows access to fields that bear the vestigial marks of prehistoric and medieval cultivation systems. On the main route, you turn off the coast path here to follow the line of a great Iron Age earthwork, known as the Bulwark. This is an impressive piece of engineering, even by today's standards, some 2,000ft (609m) in length and over 12ft (4m) high. Eventually a track leads to the serene hamlet of Penare and then across fields and down a little valley back into Gorran Haven.

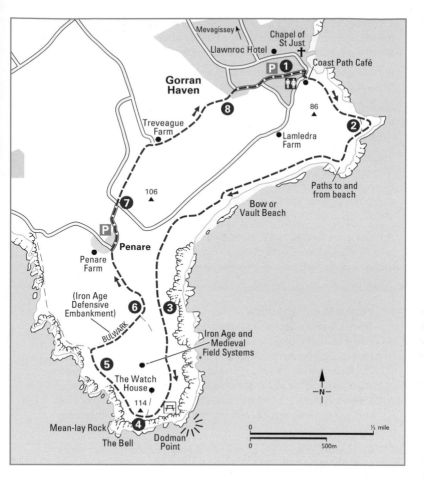

1. Turn left on leaving the car park and walk down to Gorran Haven harbour. Just before you come to the access onto the beach, turn right to walk up Foxhole Lane, then go up some steps, signposted 'Hemmick via Dodman'. Walk up some more steps, passing the Coast Path Café. Now follow the coast path ahead, past a sign for the National Trust property of Lamledra.

2. Keep to the main coast path, which goes down a flight of stone steps just beneath a rocky outcrop. At a junction marked by a coast path sign, bear right uphill, going straight ahead and through a kissing gate (the left-hand track leads down to Vault Beach from where you can come back to the coastal path again by another track that leads uphill). Where the path begins to level out, fork left and go through a gap in the hedge.

3. Go through a pair of gates and follow a path through scrubland. Keep ahead at a kissing gate by a junction signed 'Dodman Point' then eventually go through another kissing gate onto open ground. Continue on this footpath to the summit of Dodman Point.

141

4. Just before the large granite cross on the summit of the Dodman, two paths branch off right. The first leads to the Watch House. After visiting the cross take the second of these paths and continue along the coast path.

5. Turn right off the coast path through a gate signposted 'Penare' and then follow the path between the high banks of the Bulwark.

6. Keep ahead where a path comes in from the right, bear left and follow the hedged track to reach a gate and a surfaced lane at Penare. Turn right along the lane.

7. At a junction leave the road and go through a field gate signposted 'Treveague'. Follow the path across the fields and through the Treveague Farm Campsite. At the campsite gates turn right, signposted 'Gorran Haven'. Go left at another signpost and go along a drive behind a house, bearing right. Drop steadily down a path through scrub.

8. Cross a muddy area by some stepping stones, then go through a kissing gate. After a gate, follow the driveway to a T-junction with the road. Turn right and walk down, with care as there can be traffic, to Gorran Haven car park.

Where to eat and drink

There is a seasonal café at the Treveague Farm Campsite. In Gorran Haven you'll find Cakebreads, which is a shop selling snacks and ice creams and, in summer, a licensed café. On the other side of the road, The Haven serves takeaway fish and chips. A few steps away, along the coastal path, is the pleasingly situated Coast Path Café. The upmarket Llawnroc Hotel has a bistro. It is reached by walking up Church Street from the entrance to the beach, and then by going left up Chute Lane.

What to see

In Cornwall, 'hedges' are granite or slate walls bound together with earth and dense with mosses and vegetation. All along the damp lanes of the field tracks and on the embankment of the Bulwark, look for colourful plant species which thrive in these conditions. Look out for red valerian, the pink and white dog rose, the violet-coloured selfheal and the scented, cream-coloured honeysuckle.

While you're there

Explore Gorran Haven, a village with a redoubtable history. Once a busy fishing port engaged in seining for pilchards, the Haven was also visited by larger vessels trading in coal and limestone. Lime for 'sweetening' local fields was extracted from the limestone in a kiln by the beach. Visit the Chapel of St Just, the restored version of a medieval building that at one time was used as a fishermen's store.

PORTMELLON AND BODRUGAN

DISTANCE/TIME	3.5 miles (5.6km) / 2hrs 30min
ASCENT/GRADIENT	492ft (150m) / ▲ ▲
PATHS	Excellent throughout, but may be very muddy in wet conditions; several stiles
LANDSCAPE	A low coastline and rocky foreshore with fields rising steeply behind, then a deep, wooded valley
SUGGESTED MAP	OS Explorer 105 Falmouth & Mevagissey
START/FINISH	Grid reference: SX016439
DOG FRIENDLINESS	Lead required around livestock, through farm and on road
PARKING	Car park next to The Rising Sun Inn, Portmellon
PUBLIC TOILETS	None on route

Portmellon is a tiny seashore settlement to the south of Mevagissey. The authentic flavour of Old Cornwall clings firmly to the area, not least to the fishing port of Mevagissey (or 'Meva' to locals), in spite of the village's popularity in summer. There has been some unsympathetic development in Mevagissey, but the older part of the port retains a rich vernacular character.

The walk starts at Portmellon, where sturdy Cornish fishing boats, yachts and launches were once built at the Percy Mitchell boatyard. Percy Mitchell was an outstanding boat-builder who was described as 'an artist in wood'. The slipway on the seaward side of the road survives – when vessels were ready for launching, they were towed from the boatyard on a trolley, across the road and then launched from here. Just beyond the slipway, your route veers off along the route of the coast path to the delightful twin headlands of Chapel Point and Turbot Point. Chapel Point is a low-lying section of coast where the closer merging of sea with land imparts a wonderful sense of freshness and open space. The handsome dwellings on the point were built in the 1930s.

Between Chapel Point and Turbot Point is the lovely Colona Beach. Turbot Point has the alternative name of Bodrugan's Leap. The name derives from an apocryphal event during which local 15th-century landowner Sir Henry Trenowth of nearby Bodrugan is said to have leapt from his horse into a waiting boat while being pursued by Sir Richard Edgcumbe of Cotehele. The pair had been at each other's throats for years because of their divergent politics. Bodrugan supported Richard III against Henry Tudor during the Wars of the Roses; Edgcumbe's loyalties were to Henry. With the triumph of Henry over Richard at the Battle of Bosworth Field in 1485, Bodrugan was charged with treason. Edgcumbe, no doubt to his great delight, was ordered to arrest his old rival who, politics apart, had slipped easily between legitimate business and piracy for years. Off to France went Bodrugan. His lands were confiscated – no doubt to the benefit of Edgcumbe and the ruling interests of the day. From this romantic reference point you turn inland alongside a stream to reach the public road at Bodrugan Barton, site of the Bodrugan family's original house (contemporary reports describe it as being more like a 'castle').

A short walk along the road followed by a steep descent of a lane and track leads into a wooded valley from where a permissive path leads through the West Bodrugan Wood Nature Reserve. This is a rich habitat for wild flowers that include bluebells in spring, as well as primroses, celandines and white wood anemones. A particularly fine species to look for in the open marshy area beyond the woods is the yellow flag iris, a conspicuous and lovely wetland plant of early summer whose vivid yellow flowers enliven the often muted greens and browns of the valley. Look also for the southern marsh orchid with its cluster of purple flowers. Where the path down the valley ends, the sea makes its presence felt once more at Portmellon's sandy shore.

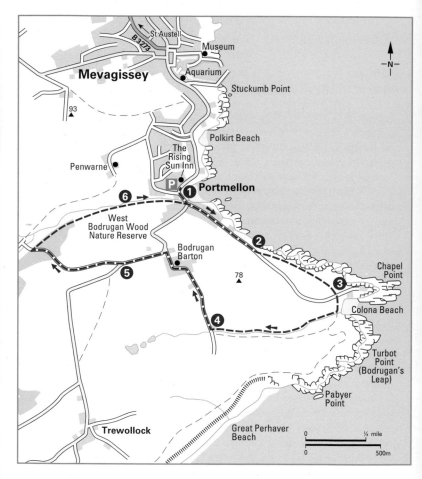

1. Leave the car park at Portmellon and walk south round the sandy bay along the seafront road. Walk uphill for 25yds (23m) and then turn off left, signposted 'Coast Path'. Continue along a surfaced road, Chapel Point Lane, lined with houses to either side.

2. In just under 0.5 miles (800m), just before a small stand of trees on the left, by a footpath sign, turn left away from the surfaced road onto the coast path (dogs on lead here). The path soon goes close to the cliff edge, so take care here. Go over a slate stile and through a gate, and then keep to a well-defined path along the seaward edge of a steep field. The path becomes a grassy track leading towards the distinctive houses on Chapel Point (private).

3. Cross a surfaced drive and follow the coast path above Colona Beach. Go over a stile behind a stone boathouse and turn right through a small metal gate. Follow a grassy path inland, between a stream on your left and a wire fence.

4. Go through a gate in front of a house and climb up some steps. Go uphill on a stony track and keep walking up straight ahead through a gate to continue through Bodrugan Barton farm. Ignore a track off to the left and zig-zag to the left of various houses. Follow the drive through an entranceway to reach the public road. Turn left and walk along the road, with care, for about 350yds (320m).

5. Bear off right down a lane. After a few paces go through a galvanised gate, whereafter the lane heads downhill into woods. Just before the lane reaches the valley bottom, turn right through a gate signed 'West Bodrugan Wood Nature Reserve'. Follow the sometimes muddy path through woods, cross a stile and reach some wooden steps up and down over a hedge leading into a field beside an open area of wetland.

6. Continue along field-edges. Go over a stile next to a gate and along a short section of muddy lane. Go ahead along a surfaced road past houses to reach the seafront at Portmellon. Turn left to return to the car park.

Where to eat and drink

The Rising Sun Inn at Portmellon is a classic Cornish hostelry where you can choose from a fine array of real ales and enjoy a pub lunch or a more substantial meal. Fish dishes are a speciality. There are particularly lovely picnic spots by Colona Beach.

What to see

The low coastline and rocky foreshore round both Chapel Point and Colona Beach are ideal habitats for birds such as the turnstone. The turnstone is a smallish bird slightly bigger than a thrush. It has mottled brown feathers, a white front and orange legs, and can often be seen working very quickly along the shoreline and among seaweed-covered rocks, searching out food with its very strong, pointed beak.

While you're there

Nearby Mevagissey should not be missed, of course. A stroll around the harbour area and the older parts of the village is a pleasure in itself, but you should also fit in visits to the Mevagissey Aquarium, located in the old lifeboat house at the harbour, and to the Mevagissey Museum, housed in an 18th-century building and full of splendid exhibits.

THE WORLD OF DAPHNE DU MAURIER AT FOWEY

DISTANCE/TIME	7.5 miles (12km) / 4hrs
ASCENT/GRADIENT	820ft (250m) / ▲ ▲ ▲
PATHS	Field paths, rough lanes and coastal footpath; can be very muddy on inland tracks during wet weather; several stiles
LANDSCAPE	Coastal fields, woodland and open coastal cliffs
SUGGESTED MAP	OS Explorer 107 St Austell & Liskeard Mevagissey
START/FINISH	Grid reference: SX118511
DOG FRIENDLINESS	Dogs on lead in fields. No dogs on beaches Easter Sunday to 1 October
PARKING	Readymoney Cove car park, reached by continuing along Hanson Drive from the entrance to Fowey's main car park
PUBLIC TOILETS	Readymoney Cove

Fowey and its environs cry out for the romantic novel, and it is no surprise that the area inspired the writer Daphne du Maurier, who lived for many years as a tenant at Menabilly House, the ancestral home of the Rashleigh family. Menabilly was the shadowy inspiration for the fictional house of 'Manderley' in *Rebecca*. The house also inspired the setting for *My Cousin Rachel*.

The walk starts from the charmingly named Readymoney Cove, a corrupted form of the Cornish *redeman*, possibly translating as 'stony ford'. From the cove you follow Love Lane, a very old cartway that rises over scarred rock slabs into Covington Wood. Soon open fields are reached and the route strikes inland along field paths and enclosed tracks. In the little valley below Lankelly Farm the path passes through a tunnel and beneath what was once a carriageway leading to Menabilly House. Beyond Tregaminion Farm and church, the long western flank of the Gribbin Peninsula is gained. Here you can divert down a zig-zag path to Polkerris Cove and beach. The coastal footpath is followed south to Gribbin Head and its crowning 'Daymark', an immense edifice erected in 1832 as a warning mark to sailors who too often had mistaken the shallow waters of St Austell Bay for the secure anchorage of Falmouth Roads further west. The Daymark was erected on land granted by William Rashleigh of Menabilly. The inscription defines the mercantile priorities of the day, the 'safety of commerce' first, 'preservation of mariners' second.

Head north from here to Polridmouth Cove (P'ridmouth to the initiated) and the heart of 'du Maurier country', from where a minor rollercoaster hike takes you to St Catherine's Point and to the ruins of the 16th-century St Catherine's Castle. The castle was part of a chain of defences built on the orders of Henry VIII as a precaution against potential invasion from France. Its lower level housed later 18th-century guns. From the high ground of St Catherine's Point there is a steep descent to Readymoney Cove.

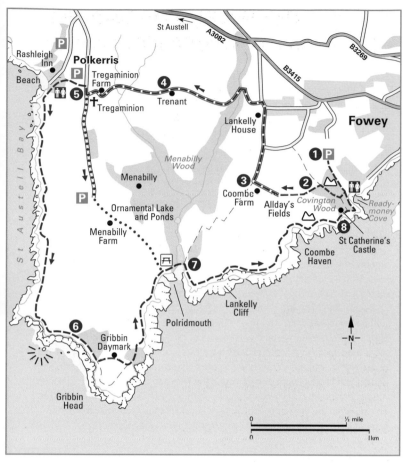

1. From the bottom end of the car park, descend the slope then turn left down The Parade. Turn right towards Readymoney Cove. Continue to the end of the road, above the beach, and follow the initially rocky Love Lane uphill on the Saints Way. At the T-junction turn right, uphill, to leave the coast path.

2. Turn left at the next junction and then climb wooden steps to reach Allday's Fields. Follow the right-hand field-edge. At a field gap follow an obvious grassy track diagonally across the field to a lane end at Coombe Farm. Follow the lane ahead.

3. At a road, turn right and continue to Lankelly House. Pass a junction on the right and follow Prickly Post Lane for a few paces. Turn off left onto a gravel drive, then keep left and along a narrow fenced-in path.

4. After the barn conversions at Trenant, cross a surfaced lane, then a stile. Keep ahead alongside the field-edge, then follow the path to a gate and a footbridge to a kissing gate and footbridge into a field below Tregaminion Farm. Bear left uphill towards farm buildings, go through a gate, keep ahead and then turn right, then left, to reach a T-junction with a road by the entrance gate to the little Church of Tregaminion.

5. Turn right and in 100yds (91m) go left into a field. Reach a junction on the edge of some woods where you meet the South West Coast Path. Keep left along the field-edge and follow the well-defined coast path for 1.25 miles (2km) to Gribbin Head.

6. Enter the wooded National Trust property of Gribbin Head. Fork right to follow the coast path through a gate and cross to the Gribbin Daymark. Go left and down a faint grassy track, then follow the coast path along to Polridmouth.

7. Follow the coast path and, at open ground, follow the seaward field-edge. Go into, and out of, Coombe Haven. Follow the path to enter Covington Wood.

8. Go right to reach the cliff above St Catherine's Castle. Pass the path to the castle, then go down steps at the first junction on the right to reach Readymoney Beach. Return to the car park via St Catherine's Parade.

Shortening the walk This shortened version of the walk allows more time to enjoy Polridmouth Cove. You can also make a short diversion south to visit the Gribbin Daymark. Follow the main walk as far as waypoint 5, from where you turn left along the road. At a car park, continue along the surfaced road, signposted 'Menabilly Farm'. Continue when the surfaced road becomes a track, and then a path that descends to reach Polridmouth Cove, used by du Maurier as a setting in *Rebecca*. Today it retains much of its picturesque character. The lake was created in the early 20th century as a pleasant adjunct to the Menabilly Estate. The house by the lake stands on the site of an old corn mill. Polridmouth's lake was made use of during World War II as a night-time decoy in a bid to protect the strategically important Fowey Harbour. Illuminations, remotely controlled to seem like carelessly exposed harbour and building lights, were placed round the lake and smaller, adjoining ponds. A rigidly enforced blackout kept Fowey in total darkness. Luckily for both, no bombs fell in the area and Polridmouth survives today with its ornamental lake intact, still striking a happy contrast with the wild foreshore.

Where to eat and drink
There is usually an ice cream and soft drinks van at Readymoney Cove during the summer. In nearby Polkerris the Rashleigh Inn overlooks the beach, and there is Sam's on the Beach (in the old lifeboat house). The Hungry Sailor Café serves artisan ice cream and cheesy chips.

What to see
The coastal fields, between waypoints 5 and 6, offer wonderful views across St Austell Bay and inland. This is the heart of the Cornish china clay industry, a vital contributor to the county's economy.

While you're there
Visit Polkerris, the small cove and beach tucked in the eastern arm of St Austell Bay. It was once a busy fishing village in the days when the great bight of St Austell Bay saw shoals of pilchard staining its clear waters purple. Today, Polkerris and the green flank of the Gribbin Peninsula stand as a counter-image to the industrial landscape of the bay's opposite shore and the china clay industry.

ALONG THE COAST FROM POLRUAN

DISTANCE/TIME	4.5 miles (7.2km) / 2hrs 30min
ASCENT/GRADIENT	754ft (230m) / ▲▲
PATHS	Good throughout. Can be very muddy in woodland areas during wet weather
LANDSCAPE	Deep woodland alongside tidal creek. Open coastal cliffs
SUGGESTED MAP	OS Explorer 107 St Austell & Liskeard
START/FINISH	Grid reference: SX126511
DOG FRIENDLINESS	Dogs on lead through grazed areas and as notices indicate
PARKING	Polruan. An alternative start to the walk can be made from the National Trust Lantic Bay car park (waypoint 4, SX149513). You can also park at Fowey's Central car park, then catch the ferry to Polruan
PUBLIC TOILETS	Polruan Quay

There are parts of Cornwall so encompassed by the sea that they seem genuinely out of this modern world. The sea, rather than the dual carriageway, is still their major highway. The village of Polruan on the estuary of the River Fowey is one such place. The village can be reached by land only along fairly minor roads that detour at some length from Cornwall's main spinal highways. Yet Polruan lies only a few hundred yards across the estuary from the bustling town of Fowey, and a regular passenger ferry runs between the two.

Prehistoric settlers found a natural refuge on the narrow headland on which Polruan stands. Christian 'saints' and medieval worshippers set up chantries and chapels in the sheltered hollows; merchants prospered from the lucrative sea trade into Fowey's natural harbour. During the wars of the 14th and 15th centuries, Fowey ships harried foreign vessels, and because of their outstanding seamanship, earned themselves the admiring sobriquet of 'Fowey Gallants'. The entrance to the estuary was protected from attack by a chain barrier that could be winched across the river's mouth from blockhouses on either bank. In peacetime the Gallants continued to raid shipping of all types until Edward IV responded to complaints from foreign merchants, and several English ones, by confiscating ships and by having the protective chain removed. Resilient as always, the seamen of Fowey and Polruan turned their hands successfully to fishing and smuggling instead.

The route of this walk starts from Polruan. It wanders through peaceful countryside. At its heart lies the splendid Lanteglos Church of St Winwaloe, or St Wyllow. The second part of the walk leads back to the sea, to the steep headland of Pencarrow and to the dramatic amphitheatre of Lantic Bay. From here, the coastal footpath leads airily back to Polruan.

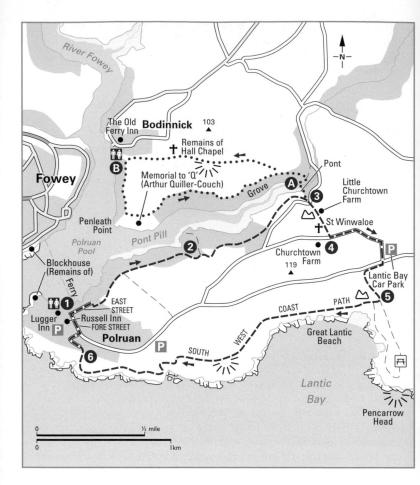

1. Walk up from the Quay at Polruan, then turn left along East Street, by a telephone box and a seat. Go right, up steps, signposted 'Hall Walk'. Go left at the next junction, then keep along the path ahead, eventually passing a National Trust sign, 'North Downs'.

2. Continue forward, eventually turning right at a T-junction with a track, then in just a few paces, bear off left along a path, signposted 'Pont and Bodinnick'. Ignore side paths to reach a wooden gate onto a lane. Don't go through the gate, but bear left and go through a footpath gate. Follow a path, established by the National Trust, and eventually descend steep wooden steps.

3. At a T-junction with a track, turn right and climb uphill. It's worth diverting left at the T-junction to visit Pont. On the main route, reach a lane. Go left for a few paces then, on a bend by Churchtown Farm, bear off right through a gate signed 'Footpath to Church'. Climb steadily to reach the Church of St Winwaloe.

4. Turn left outside the church and follow a narrow lane. At a T-junction, just beyond Lantic Bay car park, cross the road and go through a gate, then turn right along the field-edge on a path established by the National Trust, to go through another gate. Turn left along the field-edge.

5. At the fence corner, bear left towards a gate. Just in front of the gate, turn right onto the coast path and descend steeply. (To continue to Pencarrow Head go left through the gate and follow the path to the headland. From here the coast path can be rejoined.) Follow the coast path for about 1.25 miles (2km), keeping to the cliff edge, ignoring any junctions.

6. Where the cliff path ends, go through a gate to a road junction by Furze Park. Cross the road, then go down School Lane. Turn right at 'Speakers Corner', then turn left down Fore Street to reach the Quay at Polruan.

Extending the walk To extend the walk, cross the head of Pont Pill, just down from the junction at waypoint 3 on the main walk. At Pont are the remains of a lime kiln indicating that the quay here was once busy with sailing barges offloading limestone, sand and coal, and carrying away grain, timber and farm produce. Once over the bridge, at Point A, bear right along the path, which is signposted to Bodinnick. Turn left at a T-junction and climb up through the trees of the Grove and emerge onto open fields. Go diagonally left across the first field, then go through a gate and follow the next field-edge to another gate. Go along the right-hand edge of the next field and through the middle gate of three on to a track. Soon you'll pass the ruins of the 14th-century Hall Chapel. On a bend just beyond the chapel, keep ahead through a gate into a field. Keep straight on and follow the right-hand hedge to a wooden stile. Beyond the stile, at Point B, join the Hall Walk path, by a war memorial. Turn right if you want to visit Bodinnick. On the main route, turn left along Hall Walk, a 16th-century estate promenade. Follow Hall Walk round Penleath Point to where a granite memorial commemorates the novelist Arthur Quiller-Couch, who wrote under the pen name of 'Q'. He lived for many years in the area and immortalised the town of Fowey as 'Troy Town' in his novels. Eventually the path enters woodland and continues to a kissing gate into a field above the Grove. Keep ahead to find a stile and gate on the right; turn right to retrace the outward route back towards Pont.

Where to eat and drink
The Russell Inn on Fore Street, Polruan and the Lugger Inn on Polruan Quay both do good pub lunches, and Crumpets Teashop is found at the bottom of Fore Street. The Old Ferry Inn at Bodinnick is handy for lunch.

What to see
Spend some time exploring Polruan. It has retained much of its vernacular character in spite of some modern development. There is still a sense of those former sea-dominated days in the narrow alleyways of the village.

While you're there
The handsome Church of St Winwaloe, or Wyllow, has notable wagon roofs containing some original 14th-century timbers as well as many other beams added during later centuries. The side walls and piers lean engagingly to either side. In summer, there's also squash laid on for thirsty visitors. The novelist Daphne du Maurier was married here in 1932, and the church features as 'Lanoc Church' in her book *The Loving Spirit*.

TALLAND BAY AND POLPERRO

DISTANCE/TIME	5 miles (8km) / 2hr 45min
ASCENT/GRADIENT	400ft (122m) / ▲ ▲ ▲
PATHS	Good coastal footpath and quiet lanes; paths can become muddy after prolonged rain; several stiles
LANDSCAPE	Gentle coastal area with occasional low cliffs
SUGGESTED MAP	OS Explorer 107 St Austell & Liskeard
START/FINISH	Grid reference: SX236520
DOG FRIENDLINESS	Lead required in field areas
PARKING	Hendersick National Trust car park
PUBLIC TOILETS	Just before Talland Sand Beach – see waypoint 3 on walk

This walk explores the old fishing village of Polperro. The route also passes through peaceful coastal and inland sections of National Trust property between Talland and Hendersick, and the small beaches at Talland Bay. Fishing was a mainstay here from medieval times, but this section of coast was particularly noted for its smuggling activity, especially in the 19th century.

Talland's smugglers dealt in a range of luxury goods brought in from France. These included the ubiquitous brandy, as well as fine cloth and even tea. The only people who were not involved in smuggling seem to have been the revenue men. An 18th-century vicar and noted exorcist, Richard Doidge, is alleged to have been up to his dog collar in the trade. Doidge is said to have encouraged stories of ghostly hauntings in the Talland Bay area to discourage people from travelling at night. He was even said to dress up in ghoulish costumes in which he leapt out on unsuspecting travellers in hopes of sending them packing, especially if a 'run ashore' by local smugglers was on hand.

Talland Church is a high point of this walk. This is a wonderful building, part of which dates from the 13th century. Its location, tucked into a green corner out of sight and sound of the sea, matches the building perfectly. The church is built of local slate. The tower is three-storeyed and detached from the main building, although linked by a porch with an ancient wagon roof and weathered bosses. The old village stocks are set inside the porch. The interior of the church is every bit as fascinating: the fine wagon roof in the south aisle and the medieval bench ends. To the right of the door is a slate gravestone commemorating local man Robert Mark, who is said to have been a popular smuggler, and who was shot by the revenue men.

Conspicuous tourism has not detracted from Polperro's charm, and the harbour still shelters an active fleet of fishing boats. Polperro grew out of pilchard fishing from medieval times, until a decline in the early decades of the 20th century. Polperro fishermen now follow diverse methods that include trawling, tangle netting and potting for crabs and lobsters.

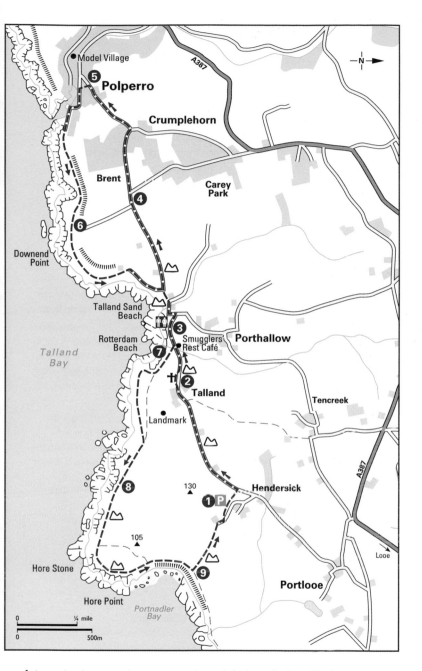

1. Leave by the car park entrance and turn left along the lane. The lane descends quite steeply once over the brow of the hill. Watch out for traffic.

2. Bear off left along a mossy path to reach Talland Church. On leaving the church turn right, through the porch exit, and follow a sunken path through the graveyard to reach some steps. Go through a gate and rejoin the lane. Descend

very steeply to reach little Rotterdam Beach, by the entrance to the Smugglers' Rest Café.

3. Continue along the road, and at a junction turn down left past the public toilets. Follow the road round right above Talland Sand Beach and past Talland Bay Beach Café. Beyond the beach, bear round left and ascend a very steep surfaced path. Where the path merges with a lane, continue steeply uphill.

4. Keep straight ahead where the lane joins a wider road. Pass Polperro School and go down a narrow lane between hedges. Turn left at a T-junction, signed 'Town Centre', and descend steeply into Polperro and to the harbour.

5. Turn left above the harbour, signposted 'Coast Path', then left again along Lansallos Street. Cross a bridge on your left by 'The House on the Props' and then turn right along The Warren. Continue along the coast path for just under 0.5 miles (800m). At a junction take the left branch and climb steeply.

6. At a guide post, turn right to follow the Coast Path. This section has been re-opened after several years of closure due to a landslip. Follow the path, passing a war memorial, to reach Talland Bay and Rotterdam Beach.

7. Opposite the Smugglers' Rest Café, turn right across the small car parking area above Rotterdam Beach. Go through a gate and climb either of two sets of steep steps. Follow the coast path along the bottom edge of sloping fields.

8. Go through a kissing gate and continue along the coast path. Go up a series of steep steps and then cross a stile by a sign indicating the National Trust's Hendersick property. Continue along the coast path, round Hore Point, going up and down some steep flights of steps on the way. Go through a gate, cross a wooden footbridge and then go through another gate. Cross a second footbridge and climb steep steps.

9. At the top of the steps, by a wooden signpost, turn sharply left, signed 'Hendersick', and follow a grassy path to reach the outer corner of a wire fence. Continue up the path to a gate. Go through the gate, continue along the path, and then go through a gate with a barn to its left. Walk down a track for a few paces, then go left through a gate and follow a path through trees. Go through the gate, bear left across a track and go up a path to the car park.

Where to eat and drink

The Talland Bay Beach Café offers delicious paninis, baguettes, pasties and sandwiches. Above the smaller Rotterdam Beach is the Smugglers' Rest Café. There are numerous food outlets in Polperro.

What to see

To either side of the coast path and along the inland hedges look for the yellow-headed celandine and the tall-stemmed Alexanders. In Polperro, check out the House on the Props and Shell House.

While you're there

Spend some time in Talland Church's graveyard. Talland has a remarkable number of dark slate gravestones, many of which relate stories of local families.

THE LOOE RIVER VALLEYS

45

DISTANCE/TIME	6.5 miles (10.4km) / 3hrs 20min
ASCENT/GRADIENT	197ft (60m) / ▲ ▲
PATHS	Good woodland, riverside paths, tracks and quiet lanes. Can be very muddy on riverside sections, several stiles
LANDSCAPE	Fields, riverbank and woodland
SUGGESTED MAP	OS Explorer 107 St Austell & Liskeard
START	Grid reference: SX249591
FINISH	Grid reference: SX250538
DOG FRIENDLINESS	Dogs on lead in fields and Kilminorth Woods
PARKING	Millpool Car Park, West Looe, across river bridge from East Looe. Looe Station, 0.5 miles (800m) from Millpool car park, reached by crossing river bridge then walking north along A387 (small car park at Looe Station fills up quickly)
PUBLIC TOILETS	Duloe; Millpool car park
NOTES	The Looe Valley Line, Liskeard–Looe. Request halts at Coombe, St Keyne, Causeland and Sandplace. Tell the conductor your destination for request stop halts; 8–9 trains daily; not all trains stop at Causeland so check in advance

The two settlements of West and East Looe were quite separate until a bridge linked them from 1436 onwards. Looe has a long history of fishing and shipbuilding, and is still a thriving deep-sea fishing port with a daily fish market. Evidence of East Looe's past wealth can be seen in its narrow lanes and alleyways, and substantial buildings such as the Old Guildhall (now a museum) and Gaol, Looe's former courthouse, dating from 1500, and the timber-framed Golden Guinea Restaurant in Fore Street. West Looe is much quieter, and overlooks St George's Island, a notorious haunt of smugglers in the 18th century, and today a marine nature reserve.

This walk begins with a short train ride to the serenity of Causeland Station Halt in the valley of the East Looe River. Once the train has gone, enjoy the tranquillity of this tiny 'one-horse' stop. The walk starts with a climb to the little ridge-top village of Duloe, famed for its Bronze Age stone circle composed of eight quartzite stones, each one representing a main point of the compass. From Duloe's Church of St Cuby, with its 13th-century tower (see While you're there) the walk drops into the valley of the West Looe River, which is followed all the way back to Millpool car park. Note that stretches of this are very muddy. The final part threads through lovely Kilminorth Woods, ancient oak woods that were once 'coppiced' and are now a nature reserve.

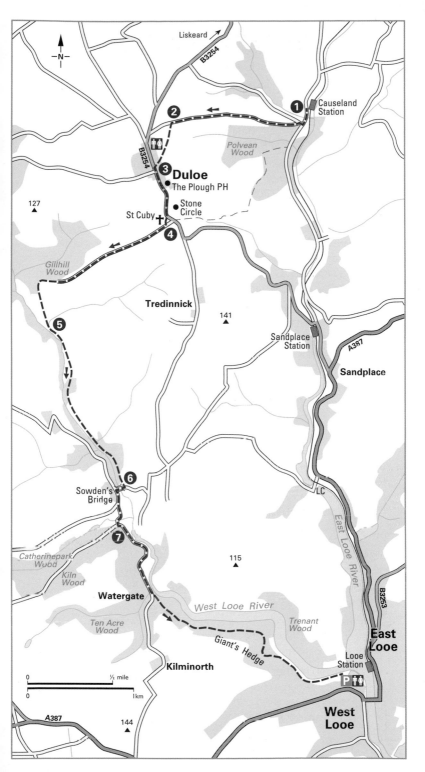

North

Liskeard

B3254

① Causeland Station

② ←

Polvean Wood

B3254

③ **Duloe**
The Plough PH

Stone Circle

St Cuby ✝

④ ←

127 ▲

Gillhill Wood

Tredinnick

141 ▲

Sandplace Station

A387

Sandplace

⑤ ↓

⑥ Sowden's Bridge

⑦

LC

Catherinepark Wood

Kiln Wood

Watergate

Ten Acre Wood

115 ▲

West Looe River

Trenant Wood

East Looe River

B3253

East Looe

Giant's Hedge

Kilminorth

Looe Station

P �person♀

0 — ½ mile
0 — 1 km

A387

144 ▲

West Looe

1. On leaving the station, turn immediately left along a quiet lane to a junction with another lane opposite Badham Farm Holiday Cottages. Turn right and brace yourself for a stiff climb for the next 0.25 miles (400m).

2. In 0.75 miles (1.2km), just before the crest, go left over a stone stile, then head diagonally across a field towards the opposite left-hand corner and a row of houses. (If the field is under crops and no right of way apparent, go round the field-edge.) Go over a stile in the field corner, bear left around the back of garages and bear left to the main road. There are public toilets to the right.

3. Go left along the pavement to pass the Plough at Duloe, preferably in time for lunch. Continue along the main road and in about 275yds (251m) you'll reach a signpost to the Duloe Stone Circle. Once back on the main road, walk the few paces to Duloe's Church of St Cuby, accessed via the cemetery.

4. From the south door of the church bear left past the tower to leave the churchyard by the top gateway into the lane (the war memorial is to the left). Turn right and follow the lane, past the school, for 0.75 miles (1.2km). Just before the tarmac ends keep ahead past a junction on the right and descend steeply into the wooded valley of the West Looe River. Go left at a T-junction.

5. Just before reaching the river, go left over a stile by a gate. Bear right opposite a gate and follow a faint, grassy path that becomes a broad track above the river. Follow the riverside way for the next 0.75 miles (1.2km). Be aware that stretches of the path are indistinct, and some areas extremely wet underfoot. Eventually reach a narrow lane at Sowden's Bridge.

6. Turn right here, then cross the bridge and follow the lane, ignoring two side junctions, going left at a three-way junction, signed 'Kilminorth and Watergate'.

7. In 0.75 miles (1.2km), turn left by pretty cottages into Kilminorth Woods. There is a choice of onward routes: either a riverside footpath, or the Giant's Hedge footpath that first climbs steeply, then follows the line of the vegetated Giant's Hedge, probably a 6th-century boundary dyke that marked out the territory of a local chieftain. Both are well signposted and lead back to West Looe. The riverside walk can be submerged by the river at one point as the tide rises. An short signed detour will guide you safely onwards if the tide is in.

Where to eat and drink
The Plough at Duloe is a classic village inn. At the end of your walk treat yourself to fish and chips on the quayside in East Looe.

What to see
In the more open valley below Sowden's Bridge, buzzards can often be seen wheeling through the sky. Further downriver, at low tide, look out for birds on the mudbanks: oystercatchers, herons and egrets.

While you're there
Visit Duloe's Church of St Cuby. The tower's lean was so acute that the top storey was removed in the 1860s. One reason given for the lean was the huge amount of smuggled goods hidden in the tower.

AROUND BODMIN MOOR

DISTANCE/TIME	3.5 miles (5.6km) / 2hrs
ASCENT/GRADIENT	230ft (70m) / ▲
PATHS	Moorland tracks and paths and disused quarry tramways
LANDSCAPE	Open moorland punctuated with rocky tors
SUGGESTED MAP	OS Explorer 109 Bodmin Moor
START/FINISH	Grid reference: SX260711
DOG FRIENDLINESS	Under control at all times; on lead in nesting season (1 March–15 July)
PARKING	The Hurlers car park on southwest side of Minions village
PUBLIC TOILETS	None on route
NOTES	There are no refreshment places to stop anywhere on the moor. You are advised to take food and drink with you. The Cheesewring Hotel & Restaurant at Minions does meals and the Hurlers Halt and Minions Tearoom serve coffee, tea and meals

The 19th-century stone workers extracted granite not only from the great raw gash of Cheesewring Quarry, but also from the wildest parts of Bodmin Moor such as the lower slopes of Kilmar Tor, on Twelve Men's Moor, where this walk leads. Cheesewring Quarry is the torn-open heart of Stowe's Hill. It takes its name from a remarkable granite 'tor', a pile of naturally formed rock that stands on the quarry's lip. The name 'Cheesewring' comes from the tor's resemblance to a traditional cider press, used to crush apples into a 'cheese'. There are many similar 'cheesewrings' throughout Bodmin Moor, but none such as this. Such formations were partly formed below ground millions of years ago, and were then exposed when erosion sculpted the landscape.

On the way up to the Cheesewring, visit Daniel Gumb's Cave, a reconstructed version of a rock 'house' once occupied by an 18th-century stone worker who was also a self-taught philosopher and mathematician. On the roof you will see a roughly carved theorem, though its authenticity is not proven. Beyond the Cheesewring, the summit of Stowe's Hill is enclosed by an old 'pound', the walls of a possible Bronze Age settlement. Relics are found at the very start of the walk, where you pass the stone circles called the Hurlers. These are remnants of Bronze Age ceremonial sites, though a later culture created fanciful tales of the pillars, and those of the nearby 'Pipers'. It's said they were men turned to stone for playing the Cornish sport of hurling on a Sunday. Beyond the Cheesewring and the Hurlers, the walk will take you through a compelling landscape, along the granite 'setts' or slabs of disused quarry tramways, and past lonely tors at the heart of Bodmin Moor.

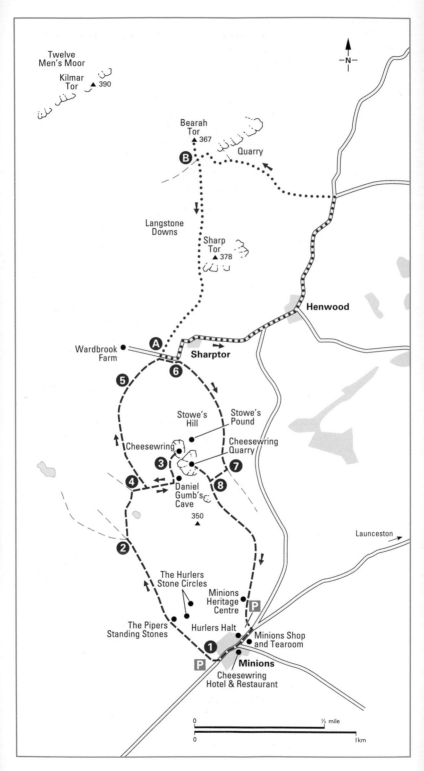

1. Leave the car park by steps at its top end. Cross the grass to a broad stony track. Turn right and follow the track, passing the Hurlers circles (there is an information board about the stone circles in the car park) on the right and the Pipers standing stones further on.

2. At a three-way junction, take the right-hand track down through a shallow valley bottom, then climb uphill on a green track towards Cheesewring Quarry. At a junction with another track, cross over and follow a grassy track uphill towards the right side of the quarry. Bear left to the nearest green hillock on the quarry edge, go sharp right, then round to the left to find Daniel Gumb's Cave. Return to the path and follow it uphill alongside the fenced-in rim of the quarry to the Cheesewring rock formation.

3. Retrace your steps towards the shallow valley bottom.

4. A short distance from the valley bottom, abreast of some thorn trees on the right and just before a fenced-off mound on the left, turn off right along a path. Keep left of the thorn trees and a big leaning block of granite and pick up the faint beginnings of a grassy track. Follow this track, keeping to the right of a thorn tree and gorse bushes. The track soon becomes much clearer.

5. The track begins to divide. At a leaning rock, split like a whale's mouth, keep right along a path through scrub and with the rocky heights of Sharp Tor in line ahead. Keep to the path round the slope, with Wardbrook Farm left and Sharp Tor ahead. Reach a surfaced road. Without going onto the road, turn right for few paces to reach a slim granite pillar.

6. Just past the pillar, keep to the right of the fence and follow a path, initially parallel to the lane, along a disused tramway.

7. About 100yds (110m) beyond some mountainous spoil heaps turn sharp right at a wall corner. Follow a green track uphill and alongside a wall. Where the wall ends, keep on uphill to reach a broad track.

8. Turn right along the track if you want to visit Cheesewring Quarry. For the main route, turn left, soon skirting left round a fenced shaft, and follow the track to Minions village. Pass the Minions Heritage Centre, a converted mine engine house. At the main road, turn right through the village to return to the car park.

Extending the walk From the main walk at Point A, go right to walk along a surfaced road. Continue downhill, through the hamlet of Sharptor, for 0.75 mile (1.2m), until you reach the pretty hamlet of Henwood. At the tiny village green, fork left (signposted 'Kingbeare') and follow the road steeply uphill until, after the Sunrising Riding Club, the gradient eases. Continue for another 500yds (457m) to a crossroads. Take the track on the left over a ford and climb steeply to a gate, which leads to an attractive area of moorland dotted with rowan, thorn, holly and oak trees and bushes. Continue up the track until just before Bearah Tor Quarry. Turn left at an old concrete shelter and pick your way across rough ground below two huge spoil heaps, until level with a lone holly tree at the left end of a third pile. Keep going along the flat, narrow path for 100yds (110m) past a thorn tree on the left, to reach a granite ramp to the left of the path, Point B. Now take a faint path that zig-zags up to the top of the ridge at the prominent 'cheesewring' of Bearah Tor, to reach a fine picnic spot with sensational views of Kit Hill, Dartmoor and the truly spectacular ridge of Kilmar Tor. Retrace your steps to Point B. Turn right for a few paces, then left downhill, passing a large granite boulder and aiming for the right edge of Sharp Tor ahead. Once there descend to a metal gate. Follow the path downhill, with a wall right, then turn right on a permissive path which leads to Henwood Lane at Point A. Turn left to rejoin the main route.

Where to eat and drink

The Cheesewring Hotel and Restaurant in Minions is a free house that serves meals, cream teas and afternoon snacks. Those with tea needs are catered for by the Minions Shop and Tearoom and the nearby Hurlers Halt tea shop.

What to see

The stone setts of the old tramways are reminders of Bodmin's stone-cutting industry, but you'll also see the remains of buildings and granite ramps from which stone was loaded into wagons. The boulders and little 'cheesewrings' of Stowe's Hill and Kilmar Tor were protected from quarrying, and on Stowe's Hill especially, near the edge of Cheesewring Quarry, you might spot a fleur-de-lys carved into boulders, a mark used to designate the limits of quarrying and stone cutting.

While you're there

Bodmin Moor was exploited below ground as well as above. Its story is told at the excellent (and free) Minions Heritage Centre in the refurbished Houseman's Engine House, once used to pump water from the South Phoenix Mine.

A STROLL THROUGH LAUNCESTON

DISTANCE/TIME	2 miles (3.2km) / 1hr 30min
ASCENT/GRADIENT	131ft (40m) / ▲
PATHS	Paved walkways and field paths, several stiles
LANDSCAPE	Townscape and grassy river valley
SUGGESTED MAP	OS Explorer 112 Launceston & Holsworthy
START/FINISH	Grid reference: SX332845
DOG FRIENDLINESS	Dogs on lead through fields
PARKING	Several car parks in Launceston
PUBLIC TOILETS	Cattle Market car park; Westgate Street car park

Launceston – easily bypassed today by those driving along the A30 – is well worth detailed exploration. It was the chief town of Cornwall during medieval times, and the county capital until 1835. The high hill at the heart of the town was probably fortified as early as the Bronze Age, but today, the striking remains of a Norman castle survive (now in the care of English Heritage) and dominate the surrounding scene. There was also an important monastic settlement here, and Launceston is the only walled town in the county. The legacy of this fascinating history is one of the most intriguing and varied townscapes in the county.

The town square – where the walk starts – has several fine buildings, including the Georgian White Hart Hotel with its 12th-century doorway, said to have been plundered many years ago from the ruins of the 12th-century Augustinian Priory of St Thomas (the latter can be visited at waypoint 4 of the walk). Other fine Georgian buildings can be seen at the bottom of Castle Street in the shape of elegant Eagle House, now a hotel, and Lawrence House a little further along the street. On the High Street evidence of the town's earlier history can be seen in the slightly leaning medieval façades of numbers 11 and 13, slate-hung and painted cream, and with an overhung third storey. Partway down Southgate Street, in view of one of Launceston's glories, Southgate Arch – a sole survivor of the medieval town's gateways – is Ching's Alley. The name celebrates a family of 19th-century wine and spirit merchants. An information board just inside the alley records some fascinating tales. The birthplace of Launceston's great literary son, the poet Charles Causley (1917–2003), is passed at the start of Riverside.

Literally towering over these layers of history is Launceston's striking castle, a round tower built on a natural mound, inside an earlier shell keep. Most of what remains today dates from the 13th century, when the Norman building was remodelled under Richard, Earl of Cornwall. The castle has never seen active service, but is an outstanding example of medieval fortification. An exhibition in the entrance building details the history of the site. Launceston is linked to the ruins of one of Devon's largest castles at Okehampton by the 24-mile (38km) Two Castles Trail.

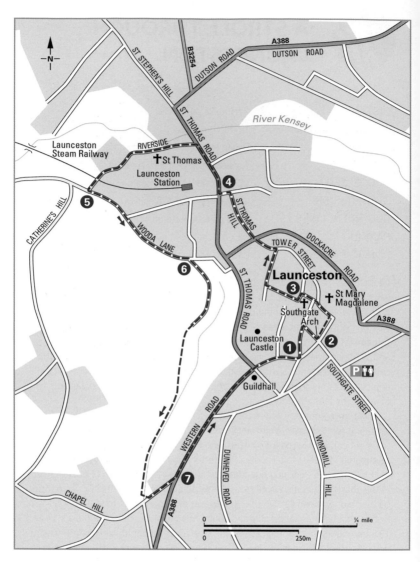

1. Start your walk by the war memorial in the town square. Leave the square by its north side (alongside the Coop) and go down the High Street. At the bottom, turn right along Church Street, then cross over into Southgate Street and walk towards Southgate Arch, passing a number of interesting buildings.

2. From the Southgate Street side of the arch go left down the alleyway of Blindhole, then follow the lane as it bears round left and passes the old market (Market House Arcade) on the left. Bear right to pass one of Launceston's finest buildings, the Church of St Mary Magdalene (see While you're there).

3. Follow Northgate Street as it curves left and downhill into Castle Street. At the bottom of the hill, on the left, is the Eagle House Hotel, but bear right to pass the National Trust's Lawrence House (see While you're there). Around

20yds (18m) further down the street, go down steps on the left, between old cottages and a new development, to reach the bottom of Tower Street. Cross Dockacre Road and go down St Thomas Hill, then turn left at the bottom and cross the busy main road with great care.

4. Turn right, keep ahead over the traffic lights, then turn left along Riverside. On the left is the Church of St Thomas; behind this lie the ruins of the Priory of St Thomas. Nearby, spanning the River Kensey, is a medieval packhorse bridge known as Prior's Bridge. Just beyond the bridge, look for a plaque on the right, celebrating the poet Charles Causley. Keep walking past a bowling green, and cross a bridge over the Launceston Steam Railway, which runs to New Mills. The track originally continued to Padstow, but closed in 1962.

5. Turn left at a T-junction. Go past a row of cottages, then, at the corner of Tredydan Road, keep straight ahead along a surfaced track, through a gate into a lane. Continue into Wooda Lane.

6. At a bend opposite cottages, go right and through a gate. Follow a path in almost a straight line for about 0.5 miles (800m), over stiles and through fields below Launceston Castle, without crossing the stream, to reach a stile and gate by a bungalow. Turn left to cross the stream and go over a stile. Turn left again and go uphill to join Western Road.

7. Continue to the busy junction with St Thomas Road. On the right is the handsome Gothic Guildhall with its wooden Black Jacks that strike a quarterly bell. Opposite is the entrance to the town's ultimate glory, its Norman castle. Continue up Western Road to the town square.

Where to eat and drink
The White Hart Hotel offers a selection of meals. Just next to the Church of St Mary Magdalene in Tower Street is the long-established Bell Inn (pasties, pork pies and Scotch eggs but no meals as such). The Little Bakehouse in Church Street is the place to go for tea, coffee and Cornish sourdough bread baked on the premises.

What to see
Look for the painted phoenix at No. 4 High Street, the old sign for a chemist, and for the lute player and angel opposite. At the corner of the High Street and Church Street admire the twisted columns and elliptical windows of No. 20, and look for 'Hayman's Pianoforte Warehouse' (now a shoe shop) in Church Street.

While you're there
The 16th-century Church of St Mary Magdalene is a remarkable building with elaborately carved stonework. On the outside is a famous recumbent statue of Mary Magdalene. An enduring local belief is that if you toss a pebble over your shoulder and it lands in the hollow of her back, good fortune will follow. The Lawrence House Museum (open April to October) in Castle Street has a fascinating collection of artefacts that tell the story of the town from earliest times.

FROM CALSTOCK TO COTEHELE

DISTANCE/TIME	4.5 miles (7.2km) / 2hrs
ASCENT/GRADIENT	164ft (50m) / ▲
PATHS	Excellent woodland tracks, can be muddy in places
LANDSCAPE	Wooded riverside
SUGGESTED MAP	OS Explorer 108 Lower Tamar Valley & Plymouth
START/FINISH	Grid reference: SX436684
DOG FRIENDLINESS	Dogs should be kept under control in Cotehele environs
PARKING	Calstock Quay car park (free), bear right at junction at bottom of steep descent into village
PUBLIC TOILETS	Calstock Quay; Cotehele House; Cotehele Quay

The River Tamar seems to take its ease at Calstock and Cotehele, where it coils lazily through the lush countryside of the Devon–Cornwall border. Today all is rural peace and quiet. Yet a century ago Calstock was a bustling river port, and had been since Saxon times. Victorian copper and tin mining turned Calstock into an even busier port at which all manner of trades developed, including shipbuilding. The coming of the railway brought an end to Calstock's importance. The mighty rail viaduct of 1906 that spans the river here is an enduring memorial to progress and to later decline, yet the Calstock of today retains the compact charm of its steep riverside location. The viaduct was built from specially cast concrete blocks – 11,000 of them were made on the Devon shore – and it is a tribute to its design that such thoroughly industrial architecture should seem so elegant today and should have become such an acceptable element in the Tamar scene.

The area's finest architectural gem is the Tudor manor house of Cotehele, the focus of this walk. Cotehele dates mainly from the late 15th and early 16th centuries. In the 17th century the Edgcumbe family, who owned the estate, transferred their seat to Mount Edgcumbe House overlooking Plymouth Sound. Cotehele ceased to be the family's main home and the house was spared too much overt modernisation. Soon the Edgcumbes came to appreciate the value of the house's Tudor integrity, and Cotehele seems to have been preserved for its own sake from the 18th century onwards. The Edgcumbes gave the house to the National Trust in 1947 and Cotehele survives as one of the finest Tudor buildings in England. The medieval plan of the house is intact; the fascinating complex of rooms, unlit by artificial light, creates an authentic atmosphere that transcends any suggestion of 'theme park' history. Cotehele was built with privacy and even defence in mind, and the materials used are splendidly rustic.

The early part of the walk leads beneath an arch of the Calstock Viaduct and on along the banks of the river, past residential properties where busy quays and shipbuilding yards once stood. Most of the walk leads through the deeply wooded Danescombe Valley, whose trees crowd round Cotehele in a seamless merging with the splendid estate gardens. The gardens support azaleas and rhododendrons and a profusion of broad-leaved trees, interspersed with terraces and a lily pond, a medieval dovecote and a Victorian summerhouse. Below the house, at Cotehele Quay, the preserved sailing barge, the *Shamrock*, and the displays in the National Trust's Discovery Centre commemorate the great days of Tamar trade. As you walk back to Calstock, along an old carriageway and through the deeper recesses of the Danescombe Valley, it is easy to imagine the remote, yet vibrant life of this once great estate and of the busy river that gave it substance.

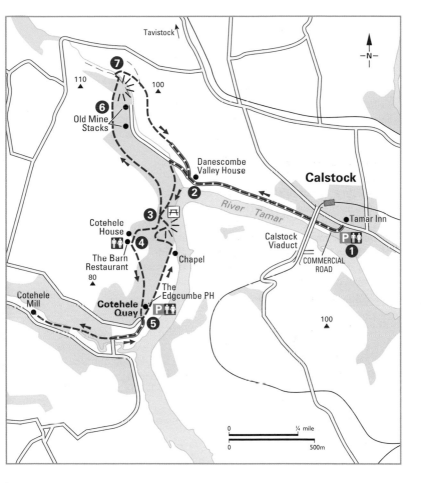

1. From the car park walk to the left of the Tamar Inn, then turn left into Commercial Road. In a few paces take the second turning left along Lower Kelly and beneath Calstock Viaduct.

2. Keep left at a fork just past Danescombe Valley House. Beyond a row of cottages branch left, signposted 'Cotehele House', and follow a broad track uphill and beneath trees.

3. Keep right (upper path) at a junction. Look out for a dovecote (left) in the gardens and then bear left. Go through a gate and turn right for the visitor reception at Cotehele House.

4. Pass through the open gateway ahead and turn left (Cotehele House right) on the road, soon branching left downhill to Cotehele Quay. (For the Mill keep ahead down the road from the Quay, then follow signs for 900yds/0.5km.) Turn left through the quay buildings.

5. Follow a path that starts beside the car park. Pass the Chapel of St George and Thomas à Becket, then a superb viewpoint over towards Calstock. At a junction, go right, signposted to Calstock. In a few paces branch left up a rising path that ascends the Danescombe Valley, bearing right at the first junction.

6. Just past a seat, bear right and descend to a wooden footbridge over a stream. At a T-junction with another track, turn left and walk up the track for about 55yds (50m).

7. Turn sharply right and go up a rising track along the side of a stone wall. Pass below a house and a junction with a path coming in left. Join the surfaced lane just before Danescombe Valley House, passed earlier. Retrace your steps to Calstock Quay.

Where to eat and drink

The Barn Restaurant is an elegant National Trust eaterie within Cotehele House. It serves morning coffee, afternoon tea and meals using a selection of local produce, and has a fine wine list. The Edgcumbe on Cotehele Quay offers similar fare. The Tamar Inn at Calstock Quay is by the start of the walk and is a traditional pub serving a range of bar meals.

What to see

The deep oak and beech woods that cloak the Danescombe Valley and all around Cotehele are a haven to wildlife. The otter, an endangered species, may still be seen along the River Tamar's banks, although you would be particularly lucky to spot one. Buzzards soar high above clearings in the trees and the neighbouring meadows. Along minor streams, kingfishers patrol their watery territory, although you'll need to keep a sharp lookout for hope of spotting them. In spring and early summer, the woods and meadows are thick with daffodils and bluebells.

While you're there

Visit the National Trust Discovery Centre at Cotehele Quay, where the story of Tamar River trade throughout the centuries is told in old pictures and displays. Cotehele Gallery has exhibitions of paintings and is located at Cotehele House. Cotehele Mill lies a short distance (signposted) from Cotehele Quay and has been restored to working order.

RAME HEAD FROM KINGSAND

DISTANCE/TIME	4 miles (6.4km) / 2hrs 30min
ASCENT/GRADIENT	340ft (104m) / ▲
PATHS	Occasionally muddy in winter on coast and field paths
LANDSCAPE	Coastal area of low cliffs and headlands, wooded and with open vegetated areas
SUGGESTED MAP	OS Explorer 108 Lower Tamar Valley & Plymouth
START/FINISH	Grid reference: SX421487
DOG FRIENDLINESS	Ponies may be grazing on the cliff tops; keep on lead where notices indicate
PARKING	Rame Head car park (adjacent to the National Coastwatch Institution lookout)
PUBLIC TOILETS	Cawsand

The Rame Peninsula takes some getting to, but this delightful corner of Cornwall offers rich rewards to the walker. You can visit the village of Cawsand, once known for prolific smuggling during the 18th and 19th centuries. Cawsand and Kingsand are said to have handled more than 17,000 casks of spirits in the one year of 1804 alone – and this in full view of England's great navy in Plymouth Sound.

Such enterprise reflects Rame's grand isolation. The peninsula, together with its neighbouring area of Maker and Mount Edgcumbe, is lodged in a corner of Cornwall marked off by Plymouth Sound to the east and the estuary of the River Lynher to the north. Roads wriggle their way onto the peninsula, from the A38, dwindling in width as they unwind deeper into the area. For centuries the Edgcumbe Estate shaped this remarkable coastal landscape, and on the route of this walk from Cawsand to the west, you follow the 'Earl's Drive', built by an Earl of Mount Edgcumbe during the early 19th century. Wealthy landowners of the time loved nothing more than transporting impressionable guests in carriages about their grand 'picturesque' estates.

The walk leads along a coastline which is layered in history, an area of immense strategic importance to the defence of Britain throughout the ages. Rame Head itself was used variously as an Iron Age fort, a lookout and as the site of a signal beacon. You can visit the summit of Rame Head and the ruin of the 14th-century St Michael's Chapel. On the west-facing coast of the headland you pass the now privately owned Polhawn Fort, once part of a sequence of defences built during the 1860s, when fear of invasion from France was rife. The cost was immense, and all to no avail. History apart, this walk entertains with its wild flowers, its breathtaking sea views and the always busy offshore traffic that sees everything from elegant yachts, to speedboats, to naval destroyers passing by.

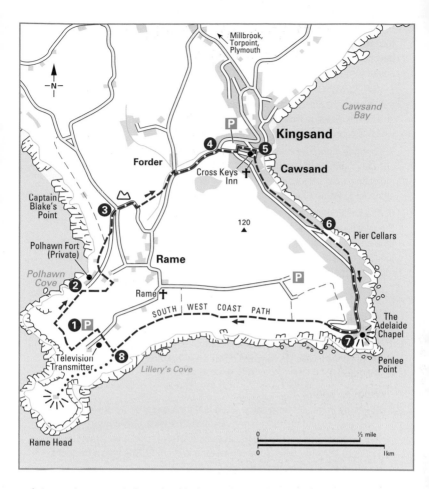

1. Leave the car park through a kissing gate at the far corner nearest the Coastwatch lookout. Head downhill to join the coast path and turn right. Cross a wooden footbridge and follow the coast path.

2. Go through a kissing gate and follow the field-edge. Go through another kissing gate and follow a path between hedges. Keep left at a fork and descend steps. Cross a driveway and go down more steps. Follow the path, and where it ends by a house, follow the driveway steeply uphill, ignoring the coastal path that leads off to the left through a kissing gate. Turn left at a junction with a metalled lane with a speed bump, and reach a junction of public roads.

3. Go half right, ignoring the lane coming in sharply from the right, and go down the main road (with care) for about 100yds (91m). Just before some buildings, go left through a kissing gate and follow the right field-edge downhill. Go through a kissing gate, turn right and, in a few paces turn left along the main road.

4. Turn right along a lane above a car park and just before a sign, 'Kingsand-Cawsand Twinned with Porspoder'. After 150yds (137m) turn left down Armada Road and follow the road round to reach The Square in Cawsand.

5. Turn right, pass the Shop in The Square, and at a junction below the church turn left along a lane, signed 'Coast Path'. This narrows to a surfaced path beyond three concrete posts. Cross a parking area beside houses and keep ahead through woods.

6. Keep straight ahead at a junction with a surfaced lane. Go past a house and then bear right along a track past some lock-up garages. Join a surfaced drive and go left. Emerge from the woods at Penlee Point above the Adelaide Chapel, which is reached down steps and a rocky path.

7. Continue along the coast path and, where the surfaced track swings abruptly right, keep straight ahead and through a kissing gate. Pass a signpost indicating a car park inland, and in another 0.5 miles (800m) pass another signpost to Rame Church.

8. At a junction of tracks by a wooden bench (radio mast visible beyond the bench), turn right and follow a grassy track to a kissing gate into a lane and to the car park opposite. Alternatively you can keep ahead at the junction to visit the summit of Rame Head. This adds another 0.5 miles (800m) to the route.

Where to eat and drink

In Cawsand's tiny Square is the Cross Keys Inn, which serves meals and pub lunches. There are other food outlets here and behind the little pebble beach, which is reached down a narrow lane from the square – The Bound.

What to see

At Penlee Point, descend some steps and then go carefully down a rocky path to find the fascinating Adelaide Chapel, a 19th-century grotto that incorporates into its fabric caves and natural rock. It was built for Princess Adelaide, wife of the future King William IV. She was a frequent visitor to Mount Edgcumbe House.

While you're there

Put some time aside to explore Cawsand and its linked village of Kingsand. The walk route takes you through Cawsand's tiny square, where a simple 19th-century drinking fountain, in the form of a globe-topped stone pillar, holds centre place.

THE CORNISH SHORES OF PLYMOUTH SOUND

DISTANCE/TIME	7.5 miles (12.1km) / 4hrs
ASCENT/GRADIENT	328ft (100m) / ▲
PATHS	Good throughout. Muddy in places in wet weather, several stiles
LANDSCAPE	Wooded shoreline of tidal creek, fields, woods and coast
SUGGESTED MAP	OS Explorer 108 Lower Tamar Valley & Plymouth
START/FINISH	Grid reference: SX453534
DOG FRIENDLINESS	Dogs on lead through fields, Mount Edgcumbe Country Park and Empacombe Harbour
PARKING	Cremyll car park. Alternatively reach Cremyll by ferry from the Plymouth side. Frequent service every day between Admiral's Hard, Stonehouse, Plymouth and Cremyll
PUBLIC TOILETS	Cremyll and Kingsand

The Mount Edgcumbe Country Park is a green oasis that flies in the face of Plymouth's crowded waterfront opposite. The two are separated by the Narrows, a few hundred yards of the 'Hamoaze', the estuary formed by the rivers Tavy, Lynher and Tamar. Mount Edgcumbe stands on the Cornish side of the river, although it was not always 'Cornish'. In Anglo-Saxon times Devon extended across the estuary as far as Kingsand, the halfway point in this walk. Today, however, Mount Edgcumbe and its waterfront settlement of Cremyll are emphatically Cornish. They stand on the most easterly extension of the Rame Peninsula, known with ironic pride by local people as the 'Forgotten Corner'. In truth Rame is one of the loveliest parts of the Southwest, let alone of Cornwall, and this walk takes you round the shores of the inner estuary, and then over the spine of the eastern peninsula to Kingsand, before returning to Cremyll along the open shores of Plymouth Sound.

The first section of the route takes you to peaceful Empacombe, where there is a tiny harbour contained within a crescent-shaped quay. It was here, from 1706–1709, that workshops servicing the building of the famous Eddystone Lighthouse were located. Behind the harbour is the Gothic façade of Empacombe House. The path follows the wooded shoreline of the tidal basin known as Millbrook Lake, then climbs steeply inland to reach Maker Church on the highest point of the peninsula. From here you wander through tiny fields to reach a track that leads in a long sweeping descent to the village of Kingsand.

Kingsand is a charming village, linked by the long and narrow Garrett Street to the equally charming Cawsand. These were successful smugglers' havens during the 18th and early 19th centuries. In Garrett Street, opposite the Halfway House Inn, look for a sign on the wall indicating the old Cornwall–Devon border. The Cornish side of Plymouth Sound was incorporated into

Anglo-Saxon territory in AD 705 to secure both banks of the estuary against Viking raids. Kingsand remained part of Devon until 1844. From Kingsand the route follows the coastal footpath along the shore of Plymouth Sound. Finally you reach the park environment that surrounds Mount Edgcumbe House, where you can visit the house if you wish and explore the lovely gardens.

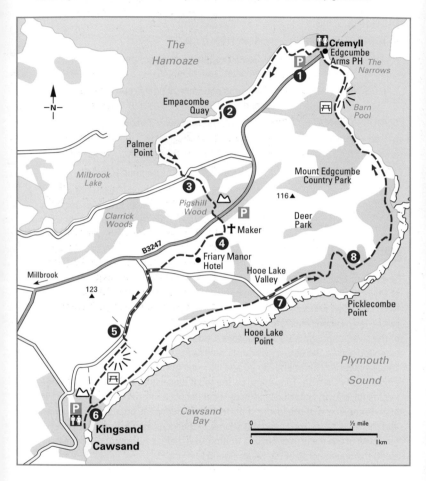

1. Find an exit by the rear of the car park next to a 'Have you paid and displayed?' sign (making sure you have first paid and displayed). Turn left along a public footpath. After a few paces, turn right at a junction and follow the path alongside the tree-fringed creek to Empacombe.

2. At a surfaced lane, by a house, keep ahead and go down to Empacombe Quay. Turn left beyond the low wall (dogs on leads) and walk along the grass, skirting the edge of the small harbour to reach a stone stile on to a wooded path. Continue round Palmer Point and onto a public road.

3. Go through the kissing gate opposite, signposted 'Maker Church, Kingsand'. Follow the track ahead for 75yds (69m) then bear right up the field, heading between telegraph poles, and through a kissing gate into Pigshill Wood. Climb